GRIEF'S COUNTRY

MADE IN MICHIGAN WRITERS SERIES

GENERAL EDITORS

Michael Delp, Interlochen Center for the Arts

M. L. Liebler, Wayne State University

A complete listing of the books in this series can be found online at wsupress.wayne.edu

GRIEF'S COUNTRY

a memoir in pieces

GAIL GRIFFIN

WAYNE STATE UNIVERSITY PRESS

Detroit

ISBN 978-0-8143-4739-3 (paperback); ISBN 978-0-8143-4740-9 (e-book)

Library of Congress Control Number: 2019955125

Publication of this book was made possible by a generous gift from
The Meijer Foundation. This work is supported in part by an award from
the Michigan Council for Arts and Cultural Affairs.

michigan
council for
&arts
cultural
affairs

Wayne State University Press
Leonard N. Simons Building
4809 Woodward Avenue
Detroit, Michigan 48201-1309

Visit us online at wsupress.wayne.edu

To want to make a fire with someone,
with you,
was all.

—Katie Ford, "All I Ever Wanted"

CONTENTS

THE BRIDE WORE BLACK

which should have been the first clue. She ambled
down the south aisle in her new cheap shoes
while the groom came down the north in the dark
blue suit men buy one of, for weddings and funerals.
Dinah Washington sang *It's very clear, our love is here
to stay*—Jesus, in a Greek play that kind of hubris
would get you castration or blinding or a raptor at the liver.
Instead everyone had omelets, made to order by a deft
and silent man behind a table in the great old mansion
on the hill overlooking the last day of the year.
A blizzard was on its way across the plains, and nobody
would get out. Meanwhile everyone smiled
and made their choices: spinach, gruyère, green onions.
Mimosas bloomed from the open bar. She flapped
and stumbled through it all: what was she doing here?
Who said her life had anything to do with strawberries
tipped in chocolate, ornate seating charts, Polish crystal
etched with names and date? Who was she kidding,
moving around the room, dazed and footsore
in those shoes, failing to see his eyes, him in the dark
suit, waiting for her to be done with this, the man standing
quiet in the cyclone's eye, slowly disappearing?

A STRONG BROWN GOD

I do not know much about gods; but I think that the river
Is a strong brown god—sullen, untamed and intractable . . .

—T. S. Eliot, "The Dry Salvages"

On my memory's retina is an open door, imprinted like a flash
image. It is a pale frame around darkness, a picture of nothingness.
I am in a warm golden-brown light, facing the door. On the other
side is sheer unrelieved night. Out there a weird and fearsome
world waits. I study myself standing there, occupying the final
instant of Before, with a terrible knowledge just beginning to rise.

✷

This story begins with a river.

It is a river of memory, though it might be memory not of what
happened but of what I was told: I am floating down the Manistee River in what my family grandly called the Au Sable Float
(named, I don't know why, for the other big river in northern lower
Michigan), which consists of the inner tube of a tire covered with
olive-drab canvas in which two leg holes have been cut. The float is
tethered to my father's waders by a rope. He is walking upstream,
fishing for trout. My feet are pushing against the rippling current.
I am maybe three or four.

By the summer of 1960, when I turned ten, my father was dead. That summer I was sent to a fifty-year-old camp for girls on a little crystalline lake among the pines southeast of Traverse City called Lake Arbutus. I would spend six summers there, taking me from ten to sixteen. Over those years my mother remarried, was widowed again, and remarried again; I inherited one set of stepsiblings and then another; I went from elementary school to junior high school to high school in three different cities and came home to three different houses with three distinct domestic cultures, three different father-men loudly or quietly determining our orbit. In that span of time the country went through a great cultural shift, and I went through puberty. In this whirlwind, those northern woods were the still place. In winter, downstate, I would imagine them silent, bare, filled with snow, and something in me feared they wouldn't be there in June. That they were—the same sunlight rippling through the spectrum of greens and breaking into diamonds on the lake, the soft, sandy soil, the smell of pine—amounted to an assurance of continuity and the possibility of return. For eight weeks I ran and swam, shot arrows and rifles, rode horses, paddled and sailed. My arm and thigh muscles rounded, my skin browned and freckled, my hair went blond. The world outside, increasingly crowded with rock bands and makeup and social strata and fashion imperatives, faded; what was real was this island of girls in the woods.

Small groups of campers were selected for overnight trips. The littlest girls were bussed with their sleeping bags to the cherry farms on the Old Mission Peninsula, which bisects Grand Traverse Bay. In a subsequent summer you might get to spend a weekend on mysterious South Manitou Island. But when you were old enough and your canoeing skills were deemed sufficient, you were tapped for what was called The Manistee—three days and two nights on the river. After canoeing the calm lake waters, the river was jazzy, both easier and more challenging. In the stern, I loved shaping the green water with my paddle, working with and against the current. I remember the sun winking through the heavy canopy of July, the long, buzzing afternoons. In the bow, less busy, I studied the whorls and eddies of the waters where I had once trailed my feet.

✳

People who loved Bob and me often said we were perfect together. On the contrary, I found us a strange match in most ways. But we had three big commonalities. We both worked at colleges—he as a student affairs administrator, I as a faculty member (although some within the academy would deny that constituted commonality). We had been fathered by American Dream men who came from nothing, made their fortunes in Detroit's industrial heyday, and in the process grew repressed, rigid, driven, and punitive, especially toward their sons. And finally, we both loved Michigan's north country. Bob's acquaintance with the area came with his first post-law-school job, at Northern Michigan University in Marquette, on the Lake Superior shore of the Upper Peninsula—*really* Up North. In fact, some Michiganders insist that Up North doesn't even start until you're over the Mackinac Bridge. But his sagas of tearing around the woods, from bar to bar, on motorcycles or snowmobiles, avoiding adulthood, shared something with my tales of tearing around the woods, from horse to lake, in Red Ball Jets, both of us creatures relishing the sense of operating outside the bounds of civilization. Among the things Bob learned Up North was the deep pleasure of wading a trout stream.

We met and became friends when we were both working at Kalamazoo College. He was married, with a young daughter and son. We merged later, after he moved to a college in western Massachusetts and his marriage ended. He quickly found his river there: the Deerfield, which runs through deep chasms in the Berkshires. I remember sitting with a book on a big flat rock overlooking the river, watching him wade the current, calculating trout behavior, casting his line. In that moment he was as centered and calm as I'd ever known him. A few years later, when I had a sabbatical, we rented a little A-frame on a small, round, perfect lake north of Amherst. I watched from the balcony as he canoed out in search of fish, over still water perfectly reflecting a ring of blazing October trees.

So now I had two dreams. Bob was the one that seemed to be realizing itself: the man who anchored me, counterweight to my histrionics and self-doubt, true and deep-rooted as a fir. The other dream was to get back Up North.

The return to paradise: the most futile human delusion. Surely I knew that. Why didn't I recognize my old tendency to look backward, yearning for what's lost? My penchant for imagined Elsewheres? Did I think reoccupying Up North would fill both needs once and for all? Or did I imagine that going back to those roots would somehow solidify a self that has often felt permeable or mutable? My dream of returning to innocence can't simply be innocent, because it flowed into disaster with the force of fate, though I don't believe in fate. The fault is mine. If only I hadn't wanted. If only I hadn't wanted so much to go back, and dragged him, my amenable Adam, into my dream of Eden. For his own good, I told myself, and this is the worst of what I live with: I had to get that man back into a river.

✳

Since my camp summers, the northwestern corner of the Lower Peninsula has been transformed by money flowing northward from the white Detroit suburbs and elsewhere. You have to know where you're going to avoid McMansions, gated communities, stacked-up condos, pricey boutiques, and chichi restaurants. My early Internet prowling, focused on lakes, revealed prices on the Arbutus-like inland lakes that temporarily stopped my heart. The one property on an adjacent lake that I actually visited, the one for sale for less than a quarter million dollars, turned out to be a sagging shotgun cottage floored in curling linoleum, smelling of mildew.

Driving north on U.S. 131 one summer day, I happened to look down as the highway crossed the Muskegon River. The river was wide, smooth, lined in thick trees. A tiny motorboat dragged a slow V upstream. I had a small epiphany: northern Michigan is laced with rivers. River property has to be cheaper than lake.

Afterward, I decided to read the way we found the place as karmic, a sign of the universe blessing my plan. Bob was now working in Colorado, and we were in our fourteenth year of peculiar long-distance togetherness. The summer of 2003, when we were both Up North, I decided it was time to get serious. After two days of trekking around several northwestern counties with a realtor, we had a more specific idea of the landscape. On Saturday we drove through the tiny village of Fife Lake and I said aloud, "I want to live here." But our explorations had also brought us to economic reality. "Let's see what happens when you raise the price a notch," said the realtor, plugging a new figure into her computer. Up popped three listings. One looked lovely, but already had a buyer. A second looked unlovely. And then came number three: a squat, funny-looking log cabin. "Five hundred feet on the Manistee," the realtor read, "outside of Fife Lake."

The next day, Sunday, we were to head back downstate. But what if this was the crooning of karma?

So we delayed our departure. We drove through the village and crossed from Grand Traverse County into hardscrabble Kalkaska County, land of lower prices. The economic collapse that would hit the rest of the country in 2008 was already happening in Michigan, especially in these rural outlands. On for five miles, through fields, marshland, stands of pine. This is Up North's unromantic backside: rooms built onto trailers and insulated in plastic; domestic ducks and geese wandering around the shells of cars; driveways where signs proclaim dire passages from Scripture—mostly the Old Testament: lots of judgment, little mercy.

The road crossed what we would learn was known locally as Rainbow Jim's Bridge, arching over a narrow point in the Manistee, and entered a tunnel of white pines. Beyond it, three parallel driveways branched out like fingers toward a horseshoe peninsula in the river.

At one of them we turned. The cabin looked much smaller than it had in the photo we'd seen on the realtor's computer. It was squat, obviously very old, built of big full logs painted an unfortunate milk-chocolate color under a green roof that had seen much better days. It sat nearly on the edge of the water. Our realtor remarked, "The codes wouldn't let it be built that close to the river today." About a hundred yards to its right was a pristine A-frame constructed of blond half logs. To the left, further off, perhaps five hundred yards through a stand of trees, was a large contemporary home. My heart sank a little; I wanted my cabin to be in the woods, not the neighborhood. Between these two places, the cabin looked very small and low and seemed to sag into itself.

But inside, it opened magically into a much bigger space: a great room with a big fireplace under a log mantle and a cathedral ceiling. A little modern kitchen with an eating area, a tiny bathroom. The sharply pitched roof made the place dark and cozy, but the whole place gleamed with the warm shine of the logs. One long tree trunk ran overhead the entire length of the living room. Upstairs a loft looked down into the great room. Downstairs a bedroom and a sunroom had been added on the river side. Outside the sunroom door was a deck. The river glimmered through the trees on the bank.

Norma, the owner, met us in a wheelchair. She'd lost a leg to diabetes, and her daughter had finally insisted she move downstate. She obviously hated the idea. I behaved as if the sale would depend on the owner's liking me. And she did. Later she said, "I knew you were the one. You and that nice man of yours."

No decision had been made. But that afternoon, driving south, without any preamble, Bob suddenly burst the silence. "What are you going to *do* with it?"

"Weekends!" I chirped. "I'm going to come up on weekends all the time, and then when you visit, we'll come up together, and we'll spend Christmas here and all summer!" Bob sighed and said I should check the property taxes. They turned out to be, like the mortgage, much higher than I was paying on my house in Kalamazoo. But investing in waterfront property in northern Michigan—how could we lose?

Later, as we negotiated over the furnishings, Norma told me she had bought the cabin with her husband, who had died suddenly shortly after they moved in. She warned me that his ghost might be around; one night she had been awakened by a chord sounding on his guitar in the empty living room. "He'll be welcome," I said happily. "I'll listen for him." A ghost—perfect.

✳

Our five hundred feet of river frontage turned out to be highly irregular and mostly inaccessible. The cabin sat high above the water, perhaps ten feet. The bank was dangerously eroded; on our side big cedars and white pines leaned out sharply over the water, roots exposed by the current. The property then sloped down to a point where Bob's son could install a dock. As the river curved away around the top of the horseshoe, the rest of our plot was swampy, overgrown, and tangled. In the middle of this little heart of darkness someone had installed a large circle of ugly white vinyl, like a gigantic children's swimming pool—to create a pond, possibly. What it created was a mosquito breeding ground coated in bright green scum. We spent hours debating how to get the thing dragged out so that the area could revert to wetland.

The cabin itself was equally irregular. Structurally, it was a nightmare. In the process of turning it from a 1940s fishing cabin to his mother's home, Norma's son had done the wiring and plumbing, both of which proved to be endless sources of mystery and frustration. Five or six experts called out to help with our water-pressure problem examined the well and the pump and shook their heads. The stunning fireplace was framed in wood, pine planks radiating in a sunburst effect, very striking—and wonderfully combustible, so that the guys who came to fix the chimney refused to touch the job until the whole thing was refaced in tile. But after we'd done it, and the guys had returned and repaired the chimney, and our neighbor had plowed our driveway so we could get in after driving up in December, we sat before the fire, watching the snow fall, Bob with his eternal dry martini with a twist, I with my Dewar's over ice, and life held itself in a tenuous, wondrous balance, like Scout, my transplanted cat, who walked the log beam above our heads.

On the deck in summer and fall, we were invisible to the kayakers and canoeists floating by, their chatter rising up from the water. Hawks nested overhead. Wild turkey paraded through the yard. On the dock I watched the green-brown water as it snaked around the bend toward me through patches of shadow and sun. I thought of the Au Sable Float and about those canoe trips, when I had wondered about the people who lived on the banks above the river. It was entirely possible that my canoe had passed this way, past this very bank, where our cabin stood. In my fifties now, I had run out of gods; what about a river god? Ever moving, ever in place—a god of paradox and dynamism. I'll make friends with the river, I thought. One of these days, I'll go in.

The sound of water washed through our days. We thought of it as the river's voice, but in fact it was the rush of water returning to water, through a drainage pipe that stuck out from the bank a few yards upriver. We fell asleep to the sound through the window above our bed, in the darkness that came down after I had the huge safety light removed. It was one of the first changes I made. Safety? From what?

✳

In December 2004, a year after we bought the cabin, my mother began to die. Over the next two weeks, efforts to stabilize her failed. Crisis to crisis, I shuttled the hundred miles between Kalamazoo, where my fall term classes were ending, and Ann Arbor, where she lived. She was often on morphine, which made her delightful and brought lovely hallucinations. But between doses her pain was terrible and one morning she begged—her voice ravaged from intubation—"Please let me go!"

So we did.

At the height of the crisis I had told Bob that Christmas at the cabin was on hold. Now I couldn't wait to be there. He flew in from where he was working now, at the University of Colorado in Boulder, and we headed north the next day. I asked him to do the driving. I can't remember ever feeling so depleted. The rolling landscape around the city of Cadillac is imprinted with the memory of that drive. I watched the low hills and sleeping fields, gray-blue, dusted with snow, flowing by as I repeated to myself that it was over, that all was well, that Mom was out of pain and had had the death she wanted. I was with Bob and we were headed to our place, where everything would be warm and quiet, and I could be still.

✳

I think it was in November of the next year that I drove up late one Friday afternoon, under a low, slate-colored sky. Saturday I woke to the windows white with the fog that had come in overnight and surrounded the cabin. The river was invisible, the trees spectral shadows.

I set about my day: grading papers, putzing around the place. From room to room something shadowed me. Outside, time seemed to have stopped; there was no change of light from hour to hour. I couldn't shake it; I felt surrounded, removed from my kind and the life I was living to some other place of silence, isolation, and vague dread.

Watching a movie didn't help. Nor did music, scotch, the nightly call from Bob, or sleep. On Sunday morning the air lightened only slightly and the fog was still wrapped tightly around the cabin. Hardly able to breathe, I gave up. I packed hurriedly and drove the five miles to the village. When I turned south onto 131 and picked up speed, the oppressive weight lifted immediately. In the space it left behind, I understood what had held the cabin in its thrall. "Death," I whispered. I had felt its presence, strong and steady. I had never experienced anything like it.

I didn't tell Bob any of this. I banished it to some outer reach. The cabin was our stake in a new life. If the cabin was where I would die, so be it.

✳

In August 2007, I was heading into a sabbatical and Bob, at last, into retirement, after ten years in Colorado. I rented out my Kalamazoo house so we could spend the year at the cabin. I had a book to write; he had major plans regarding logs and gardens. In that glorious autumn, while I covered the loft in index cards, stacks of paper, sticky notes, and legal pads, he arranged for a truck approximating the size of a T. rex to drag seven cords of wood down our driveway, sinking into the soft, sandy soil. He then proceeded to submit them to his brother's splitter, a frighteningly powerful and ungodly loud machine. Bob and Brian treated that splitter like it was a ferocious deity. The woodpile grew apace, and despite my testosterone jokes, I recognized a supremely practical, healthy alternative to therapy when I saw one. Not to mention that there was now not the remotest chance that we would be cold that winter.

One afternoon in late November, Bob was at his computer in the sunroom, at the ugly desk I'd dragged out of Goodwill for $15. I was in the kitchen. Suddenly he said, without turning from the screen, "Joe's dead."

The email with the news came to a listserv of Bob's high-school buddies. The message didn't say how Joe died, which is how we knew. The last time Bob had spoken with him, Joe confessed to feeling very depressed, unhappy that at sixty-two his life was stuck—no family, no woman, scraping together a living in film and TV as a grip and sometime producer. Behind him trailed a long history of depression, psychotherapy, and drugs—legal, illegal. Bob always urged him to visit, to call. There was no room for shock at the news; everyone who knew Joe had seen this as a possible ending for his story. The first time I met him, I saw it immediately—that gray miasma of persistent depression.

Bob called Joe's sister. As they spoke, it grew dark. I lit candles around the living room, a nightly ritual Bob regarded with disapproval, given that we lived in a pile of logs. When he hung up, he wept. "He did it just like Joe," he said. He had mailed letters to family and friends, saying that he could not face another Thanksgiving, another Christmas, another birthday. He had sent a note to the local police precinct, a block away, so that his body would be found. And he had strung up water bags to keep his cats' water dishes full for several days. Then he had ended his life.

I dropped down beside Bob on the sofa. Out the window, I could see our neighbor's Christmas lights, visible through the trees. As we sat, I made some kind of inchoate, silent prayer for Joe's wandering soul. We held each other. The light of the candles reflected in the dark windows seemed like a protective ring of fire holding the night at a distance. *We're safe*, I said to myself. *We're here together, safe.*

✳

That year's Christmas tree was our best. After hours of fruitlessly searching for the tree farms I was sure should be ubiquitous in those parts, we found it immediately at a little corner lot in a nearby town. A tall, soft, very fresh Douglas fir it was, reaching up past the beam across the living room ceiling. The day after Christmas we sped down to Kalamazoo, and on New Year's Eve morning we were married, after eighteen years together (exactly), among a small gaggle of family and friends. We sealed it with two thick gold bands. Bob's was the ring his father had worn when he married the love of his life, his second wife. I wore my paternal grandmother's ring, inscribed from her husband on the inside in delicate late Victorian script.

The wedding felt awkward to me, as if sound and picture were out of sync. I couldn't quite settle into my body or into the present moment. A blizzard was on the way, so the party dispersed in the early afternoon. We spent the night at an expensive lakefront hotel some thirty minutes north of Kalamazoo. The snow started when we were at dinner, thick and heavy, and kept on all night. New Year's Day dawned weirdly dark and never brightened. The small naked trees, black against the obliterated lake, looked eerily twisted. In the pictures I took that morning, the air is dark blue, like night. All I wanted was to be back at the cabin, in my sweats, in the ugly, bulbous, off-white leather recliner I'd bought from Norma.

And there I spent most of the winter, when I was not upstairs in the loft writing. The book came quickly, and most often, when Bob switched on NPR at 4 p.m. to indicate that the workday was over, I closed the computer with satisfaction. When the long winter gave up at last, we would see what the river was like in spring. We would spend a full glorious northern Michigan summer here. Then I would head down to the other life that waited for me, and Bob would toggle between cabin and Kalamazoo. We would investigate a bigger house there, as we both knew the cabin would never be our permanent residence—too ramshackle, too small, too far from family and friends. I would think about gearing down to part-time at the college, easing toward retirement. The days of pouring my entire life force into the drama of teaching and the intense life of a small college were over. My writing and this person now called my husband: more of my time—my attention, my imagination—now would flow into this life.

My stepfather, my mother's husband for nearly forty years, had tipped into decline immediately after her death, and died in mid-January. It felt like a cover closing on a book. I was no one's child now, for the first time. And I was no one's mother. I was a free agent, floating through the cosmos at the age of fifty-seven. What a moment to become someone's wife, to become as connected as I could ever be.

✳

One evening a week or so later, I was sitting at the kitchen table, sipping my scotch, watching Bob's preparations for dinner: precise, focused, fussy, timed like a military operation, ingredients measured and arrayed in small bowls, pork roast (his specialty) laid out on a board, ready to roast with rosemary on his small rotisserie grill. I was saying something when Bob turned from the counter and slid slowly to the floor, rolling onto his back. His head didn't strike the floor—at least, I think it didn't; this happened in slow motion, soundlessly. His eyes were open, bright as ever, but unseeing. I called his name, shook him by the shoulder, called his name, over and over. My mind raced around the room and out the window: I was alone here, five miles from a tiny town with no medical facilities, twenty miles from a larger town where perhaps there was an emergency vehicle. I was alone. The neighbors in the A-frame next door had moved and left it vacant. I didn't have a number for the neighbors on the other side, in the big contemporary. I was alone. I couldn't get Bob to my car by myself.

And then he was back, seeing me. I kept saying his name. I helped him up, and he asked what had happened. He was fine, he said, bemused. No pain anywhere, nothing. I led him to the living room sofa and sat with him, my heart drumming. He remembered nothing of falling or the preceding moments, and he had no aftereffects.

He reminded me that this had happened once before, unwitnessed by me—at a guesthouse in Key West. He had come into our room from outside, looking for a Band-Aid. He'd fainted or something, he told me, and struck his forehead on a planter; there was a small cut. He'd sworn he felt fine, not even a headache. Maybe, we'd theorized, he'd gotten out of his chair on the terrace too quickly.

Now I extracted a promise: the next day he would make an appointment with a doctor in Traverse City. We would get to the bottom of this. He was quizzical, even amused; but I was crying now and couldn't stop—big, heaving sobs. "I'm fine, hon, really!" he kept saying. He was holding me now, worried. My weeping subsided, but the terror was still in me, unexorcised, rising from some bottomless well, and the sobs rose again. Bob kept slipping away from me, before my eyes.

✷

It was a running joke between us, my problem with separations. Weirdly, in our long commuter love affair, my leaving him occasioned more grief for me than his leaving me. I think that somehow the image of him alone, left behind, pulled strings strung tighter even than my fear of my own aloneness. I remember driving east out of the Berkshires in our early days, weeping until I was well over the New York border. I recall a fairly embarrassing scene in the airport in Santa Barbara, where his parents lived, when I was flying home by myself. My pièce de résistance, however, came in a hotel lobby in Boulder where we were awaiting the shuttle that would take me to the Denver airport. He told me he needed "to use the restroom," as he always said in his decorous way, and vanished. The shuttle arrived, and my suitcase was hoisted aboard. A sheer, irrational panic lurched up from nowhere: I would have to board the bus immediately, it would leave momentarily, and Bob was gone. I went to the door of the men's room and called his name repeatedly. No answer. Finally I opened the door and set one foot inside, calling loudly, imperatively. "Yes?" said his amused voice from one of the stalls. "I'll be right with you . . . " By the time he emerged, chuckling and regarding me as if I were deranged, I had realized that the shuttle's departure was not imminent. We waited at least ten more minutes, which he filled with scatological drollery, riffs on my absurdity. He was already concocting a version of this scene to tell for the rest of our lives. I was suitably humiliated, but I was also taken aback by the intensity of my fear, shooting up from underground like a geyser in the space of a breath.

✳

In Michigan spring demands faith. It advances, then retreats. It seems to me it came especially slowly that year, though the fact is that I had never watched it come so far north. We both had full-blown cabin fever.

By the middle of April Bob was well into ongoing medical tests, none of which provided anything close to an answer for the losses of consciousness. By then the last crusty, dirty snow had vanished, and the air softened and freshened. The sunlight was warmer, even if the days stayed chilly. And the birds came back in the wondrous diversity we'd discovered at the cabin. We'd put feeders out and had the bird book handy to identify newcomers. After the first onslaught of raccoons, Bob brought the feeders inside nightly. For Christmas, he had bought me a new industrial-strength, squirrel-proof tube feeder. Where did I want it? I said I wished it could hang from the big old white pine at the edge of the river, about twenty feet from the deck, but the branches were too high. Ever one to rise to a challenge and always one to find the most complicated way to accomplish anything, Bob hooked up a Rube Goldberg rope-and-pulley apparatus by which a bird feeder could be hung on a branch out over the river and hauled back down and in for refilling. I hated the look of it, a fact I didn't mention, and I also thought it was dangerous, a fact I did. Even to work the contraption one had to lean out over the high bank.

By the first week in May, the day lilies whose bulbs I'd shoved down into the gravely soil were sending up shoots, and the trees were greening up. Nights were still too cold for open windows, but afternoons were warm enough to sit on the deck. The end of my book was clearly in sight; I would finish a draft in early summer, well before I headed back to my Kalamazoo life.

My habit that year was to allow several errands to accumulate and then, at a natural pause in my writing, to spend a day getting them done in Traverse City, forty-five minutes away. On May 8, a Thursday, I left in the morning and got home in late afternoon, just in time for cocktails on the deck. We sat at the picnic table Bob had installed, he with his martini, I with a gin and tonic. At the bird feeder closest to us, a big rose-breasted grosbeak appeared, the first either of us had ever seen. The coming summer seemed to hum in the distance.

We ate dinner and watched Tim Burton's *Sweeney Todd*, all raspberry-colored blood and steampunk melodrama. It ended at about 9:45. Bob said he was going out to bring in the bird feeders. He wore his gray sweats and the L. L. Bean slippers I'd bought him several Christmases ago, now flattened at the back into slides. I went to the bathroom to brush my teeth and wash my face.

When I came out, the door from the sunroom to the deck stood wide open. It was a heavy, full-frame glass door with little birds etched on the top. I had come to resent it; it had to be tugged open and pulled shut hard every time one of us went out or came in, as we did constantly. On my list was to arrange to have a screen door installed, one that slammed behind you, as a cabin door should. I glared at the door, wondering why Bob had left it open to admit all manner of nightlife. He was taking a long time, I noted. The night seemed very quiet.

I sat down to write a quick overdue thank-you note to his sister, but halfway through the first sentence I stopped, rose, turned, and faced the empty doorway again. Deep inside me was an inkling that I had just entered a different world.

A few seconds later, outside in the dark, first calling his name and then screaming it, I already knew the end of this story. The Christmas bird feeder hung out over the water from the limb of the white pine. At the foot of the tree lay a slipper. The cosmos roaring up inside me, I went to the brink and looked down, knowing I would see its mate there at the base of the bank, at the edge of the water.

The next hour was full of sound and motion—my shrieking, lights going on across the river, neighbors' voices, flashlights, police, tracker dogs. At one point I looked down from the bank again and, knowing it was useless, slid down into the cold tumbling river. The current pulled my feet out from under me and my head went underwater. I grabbed for a thin branch hanging low over the water. I wasn't going with him. I regained my feet and flailed downstream toward the dock.

They found him downriver around the horseshoe's bend by the neighbors' dock. For the next hour, as they tried to force life back into his body, I waited in the cabin with some neighbors. Shortly after midnight the troopers—young, buzz-cut, stiff, no experience of such duty—came back to the cabin. *He's gone*, I said, before they could speak their word, *deceased*. The rest of my life was already moving in on me.

This story ends with a river. But, like the river, it doesn't end. It runs on and on.

GHOST TOWN

Gold Hill is sometimes labeled a ghost town,
which is an inaccurate designation.

—Wikipedia

There are four ways to get to Gold Hill. You can take CO72, aka the Peak-to-Peak Highway, to Gold Hill Road, which comes into town from the west. It's a long, dusty few miles that will take you past the Sacred Mountain Ashram, established 1974, and the Colorado Mountain Ranch before curving to the right, down into town. If you decide against turning off, by the way, the Peak-to-Peak will take you to Nederland, a bustling mountain town with amenities like restaurants and a movie theater. Nederland is the home of the excavated frozen body that is celebrated in an annual three-day festival in March called Frozen Dead Guy Days.

Alternately, you can reach Gold Hill from Left Hand Canyon, to the north, named for the Arapaho leader memorialized in various ways around Boulder County, whose name in his own language was Niwot. This is not a popular route for a variety of reasons, one of which is that to go from the canyon up to the town requires you to use a road called Lickskillet, which holds the honor of being the steepest charted road in the United States, closer to perpendicular to the earth than any road has a right to be. Legend has it that the name comes from the greasy skillet dangled before the pack mules to entice them up the hill in the mining days. This road is completely closed by November. I was constitutionally unable to drive up or down it at any time.

Naturally, the two busiest routes come from Boulder. One via Four-Mile Canyon runs flat out of town and then leaps up into the mountains, winding wildly. One hairpin turn deep in a canyon takes you through the town of Salina, a handful of little houses wedged against the rocks, buried in shadow. At the turn leaving town stands a cabin with the unfinished, jury-rigged Rube Goldberg quality I would see repeatedly in the hills above Boulder. A striped blanket serves as a curtain over the front window. The road then rises sharply, swings through another tight hairpin, flattens out, and heads into town.

The other popular route, from the east, takes Sunshine Canyon past homes that run from substantial to weird to palatial, and then finally up a series of hairpins around Horsfal Mountain. For months I only heard that name, never read it, so I thought it commemorated a tragic equine accident. After climbing sharply, you level out onto the Lower and then Upper Shelf Roads, which look and feel exactly like their names. They are (barely) two lanes wide: mountainside on the left and on the right a sheer drop of about a thousand feet into the canyon. No railing, no berm, nothing but nothing. If you're ever going to make friends with this route—which is by far the prettiest and possibly the most expeditious—you simply have to keep your eyes focused straight ahead and trust that there is not a monstrous propane truck coming around the next bend. When you can drive it at night, or in snow, you're a local. Your reward comes as the Upper Shelf curves to the left and the town is spread out beneath you in a hollow. At the edge of town, you see the sign:

GOLD HILL

```
EST. ---------------- 1859
ELEV. -------------- 8463
POP. ---------------- 118
---------------------
TOTAL ------------- 10440
```

✳

My route to Gold Hill was longer. It took a sharp turn just before I turned forty, when I led Bob up the stairs to my bedroom for the first time in the early hours of 1990. Ten years later it merged onto I-94 west and then, past the snarl of Chicago, settled onto I-80.

I still feel the beats and rhythms of that first drive, which seemed like some mythic pilgrimage. I remember crossing the Mississippi at midday and then, at the end of the afternoon, the Missouri, thinking about the potency of rivers, both as historical forces and as symbols of transition, as passages and boundaries. I remember spotting the Comfort Inn just beyond Omaha where I would unfold myself, crank up the air-conditioning, and call Bob.

Day 2 was a state of mind called Nebraska, bright and hot and endless. Green Midwest morphing slowly into dun-colored West; cottonwoods crowding around a river; signs about pioneers and Buffalo Bill churning up all the mythology of the American West in which I marinated as a kid. My car became a little silver boat pulling across the great archipelago, Grand Island to Kearney to North Platte to Ogallala, and finally, at midafternoon, Julesberg, turning onto I-75, which cuts southwest into the hard brown landscape of eastern Colorado.

There was a moment somewhere in those dazed late afternoon hours. On subsequent trips I tried unsuccessfully to find it again. A long bank of blue clouds has lined the western horizon, for how long I don't know. Suddenly I understand these are not clouds but mountains, rising up in front of me. It feels like revelation. I think of the western migrants of the nineteenth century, how they saw the Rockies reveal themselves: for some, a monumental barricade they must gird themselves to surmount; for others, as for me, the blessed end of the road.

✳

In the eighteen years of our peculiar togetherness, the longest period Bob and I actually inhabited the same space was a little under two years. This period followed the first four years of our relationship, when he was the vice president for student affairs at a small college in western Massachusetts. At the point where I was applying for sabbatical research positions in that region, his misery on the job had been steadily increasing. In one of our nightly phone calls he stunned me by announcing that he was resigning and applying for admission to the graduate education program at UMass in Amherst. We hadn't spoken about living together, but suddenly there we were, in a modified A-frame on a pristine lake north of Amherst, for ten months.

Then we moved back to Michigan. The plan was that Bob would live with me, finish his degree, and look for jobs. I went back to work in September and he took over the house. For the first time in living memory, it was cleaned regularly, the refrigerator was stocked, repairs got done, and when I got home at night I was greeted with the smell of dinner cooking. The cats were fed and let in or out as they demanded, the house was filled with music or *All Things Considered*, and, as the weather cooled, the fire was lit. It goes without saying that logs were ordered and split as needed.

But this domestic idyll was more complicated for Bob than for me. Never belligerently masculine, he was basically a conservative man and still took a lot of his cues from a very conventional 1950s gender template. It took me a while to understand that being unemployed and broke and looking after a house might unsettle him.

"I just need to feel I'm making a contribution."

"Are you kidding? My house is clean! Someone makes me dinner! The laundry gets done and my underpants are *folded*!"

"I know, hon, I just have to get used to this. This isn't something Bud would understand."

Bud, his father, was a driven, self-made man of very conventional and unexamined values. How a man should live his life was written in stone for him. A businessman himself, he never got over the fact that Bob got a law degree but never practiced law. A college vice presidency somehow didn't measure up; in Bud's world, there was business, law, or medicine. I was coming to understand that Bob's leap off the career track in Massachusetts was a remarkable and brave departure from the script. And it also involved an economic risk; he had drawn down his retirement funds twice now after leaving jobs, and he had debts. Nasty hired guns started calling on behalf of his creditors.

So when Ron's offer came, there wasn't really any question of what Bob should do. Ron, his old buddy from Northern Michigan University, where they'd begun their careers together, was now vice chancellor for student affairs at the University of Colorado at Boulder. And he had a problem: a five-year grant from the Robert Wood Johnson Foundation to support a public-health approach to alcohol abuse needed a principal investigator quickly. Would Bob take the job? Could he come right away?

Irony abounded: no one loved a martini more than Bob. He was famous for it; it was his trademark. He was an absolute purist; the martini culture that broke toward the end of the century, with its colors and flavors and flourishes, made him sniff and grimace. After he asked the waiter or bartender, "May we know your name?" his next utterance and accompanying hand gestures would be unvarying: "Bombay martini, very dry" (hands flat, parallel to the floor), "up" (hand fisted, thumb extended upward), "with a twist" (thumbs and forefingers of each hand twisting an imaginary lemon peel in opposite directions). No one was more particular as to his gin, his vermouth, the temperature of the glass and the liquor, or the way the lemon rind should be twisted—or loosely knotted, a later touch. The pristine, almost feminine delicacy I sometimes saw in him emerged when he poured a martini. No one honored cocktail hour with greater devotion. And now he was going to take on the legendary alcohol culture of CU Boulder.

"Remember how we said maybe the next job would bring you closer?" I said. "Colorado is not closer."

So I was going to lose him again. And it would be for ten years, not the promised five. And then forever.

✳

I had been to the Northwest, but that's not the West. I was shocked by how suddenly the mountains rise from the plains, as if shoved by some titanic force—as of course they were, in a great mashing and collapsing of tectonic plates. The Flatirons, the striated trinity of rock formations directly above and behind Boulder, suggested to me monumental hands pushing west. No foothills, just the plains and then the mountains, city roads S-curving quickly up canyons and around hills. It's a violent landscape, and to me a very masculine one, hard and brown and so dry you quickly understand the suddenness and virulence of deadly fires. You feel the dryness immediately in your mouth and your skin, and you notice how carefully people conserve water. Coming from a blue-and-green landscape, a state surrounded on three sides of two peninsulas by huge freshwater seas, I felt far from home, landlocked, and, of course, breathless. Colorado was another realm altogether.

When I first visited Bob the summer after he took the job, he was living in college housing, which is to say a concrete-block one-bedroom apartment floored in old brown linoleum with a refrigerator whose little freezer had to be defrosted by hand every week. It came furnished with black vinyl sofa and chairs, a decent double bed, and a dinette set. To Bob, this was perfectly fine—cheap but utterly satisfactory. To me it felt like a cell at a minimum-security facility.

While he was at work I read and wrote and hiked around town. Sometimes I drove up Boulder Canyon to one of the outlook spots with picnic tables. I loved the wide silence, the air smelling of white sage, but I could never quite relax. Big signs announced, "YOU HAVE ENTERED A MOUNTAIN LION'S HOME" and offered instructions about how to behave if confronted by the resident. So you're not only terrified but abashed by your rudeness in barging into someone else's abode. I was nearly always the only human around and I couldn't shake the feeling that I was being watched. One day I decided to hike at the Boulder Reservoir, but a man returning to the parking lot as I was leaving it said, "Be careful, some guy thinks he heard a rattler in there." I tried to keep walking, but approximately eight feet down the path I gave in and swiveled back toward the car.

On weekends Bob and I hit the laundromat, defrosted the freezer, and shopped for food. On Saturdays at the lush Boulder Farmers' Market, a brief walk away from the apartment, I always felt like we were playing in different musical keys or time signatures. For me the whole point was to luxuriate in the flowers and produce, consider the jewelry, and hit at least two food carts, probably Asian and Latin. Somehow the market brought something different out in Bob. He became Sherman marching to the sea, treating the ravishing corridor of market stalls as the local Safeway: grab what's on your list and get out. It all came to a head very quickly one Saturday.

Me, stopping his forward momentum: "Look at those green beans! Let's get some."

Him, impatiently and loudly: "You got a *plan* for those beans?"

I believe we went home separately. I later treated him to a detailed discourse on the point of farmers' markets, the value of experiencing things in common, and the relative unimportance of knowing exactly what you will do with green beans when you buy them. Within a short space of time we were both laughing. Bud had made an appearance once again. "You got a *plan* for those beans?" became a watchword whenever this Patton-like approach threatened to swamp something small and lovely.

Sometimes we took exploratory trips in Bob's 1980s maroon Oldsmobile—an ugly beast, long and low, the size of a boat, with maroon velour seats. He had been reading Colorado history since his arrival, telling me about the young women called Bluebirds who spent their summers on the Front Range. One Saturday he said, "I want to find this place Gold Hill."

We drove up Four-Mile Canyon for about a half hour, creeping around hairpins and up sharp grades, veering toward rocks. Ragged deer paused in their grazing to watch us. Finally we emerged onto a wide, graded dirt road that took us into what appeared to be a kind of camp, a collection of ramshackle cabins and other structures lining a small grid of rocky dirt lanes on a flat surrounded on three sides by high hills.

I was lost, utterly disoriented. I didn't understand what it was. "Town" truly did not suggest itself. The place was inscrutable. My mind had no frame for this picture. Bob maneuvered the SS *Olds* around impossibly tight corners, up and down ruts and mounds, over boulders, past an inn that apparently served dinners and a tiny general store. "What's—what *is* this?" I kept asking.

"It's Gold Hill," he said helpfully.

I thought a big A-frame up on the flank of the biggest hill, looking down over the grid, might be some kind of headquarters, some central camp lodge. Otherwise, I might have believed we'd entered a time warp. A western could be filmed here, I thought, without much set dressing.

✳

In November 1858, far away from bloody Kansas and the rumbles of war back east, a gaggle of prospectors from the Midwest made a base camp at the edge of what would be the city of Boulder. In January, of all months, they headed up the old Arapaho path into the mountains. Three thousand feet up, in a stream at the base of a hill, they found gold. The road they subsequently made from the footpath in order to transport their treasure would be called Gold Run. In March 1859 the site was established as Mountain District #1 in Nebraska—Colorado would not be established as a distinct territory for another two years. In May, up on top of the hill, they struck a gold-bearing vein, and in June a group including David Horsfal hit the mother lode nearby, and the Colorado gold rush was on. The site reputedly produced $100,000 worth of gold the first year, drawing a minor flood of hungry hopefuls. On the flats atop what became known as Horsfal they planted something like a town and christened it—what else?—Gold Hill.

The town grew to the point where the official census registered 423 males and 65 females. But the settlement's existence was always precarious. Exposure to wind and weather took its toll, and fire swept through in 1860, destroying most of the town. The following year the surface deposits of gold began to dry up, and remaining residents headed for the plains or other shiny dreams. The census of 1870 recorded only seven citizens, and Gold Hill became a specter of itself. Then, in 1872, the second chapter in Colorado mining history opened with the discovery of tellurium—only the second known source of the ore in the world. The population of the town boomed to close to a thousand. A newspaper was founded, as well as a school under the supervision of one Hannah Spaulding. The Grand Mountain Hotel was built, later renamed the Wentworth for its owner. Eugene Field, so-called poet of childhood, author of "Wynken, Blynken, and Nod" and "Little Boy Blue," immortalized the place in "Casey's Table d'Hote," a long poem in unbearable "western" dialect. The telegraph arrived in 1875, statehood for Colorado the next year, and electricity a decade later. Ghostliness threatened in the form of a disastrous fire in November 1894 that came close to destroying the town once again. But the wind shifted and snow blessedly fell, and Gold Hill staggered into the new century.

With the establishment of the national parks and also the notion of the salience of evacuating the physically and morally grimy eastern cities in the summer, western tourism bloomed. Clarence Darrow came through town and stayed at the hotel. In 1920, thanks to a brainstorm on the part of one of Jane Addams's protégés at Hull House, the hotel was bought by the Holiday House Association of Chicago as a resort for young professional women—nurses, teachers, social workers—on western tours. Bluebirds, they were called, and the hotel became the Bluebird Lodge. As the mining industry dwindled and the national economy slowed and then crashed, Gold Hill began to vanish yet again. But the two-room school stayed open and today is the oldest continuously operating school in Colorado. The locals have fought its closure on numerous occasions. Somewhere near the point where matter becomes myth and history grows haunted, Gold Hill lives.

✳

I don't know when I grasped that Gold Hill was real, a functioning community with families and that historic school. But it got realer when Bob was asked to house- and dog-sit up there by a CU colleague, a guy he'd met on the handball court. This friend's name was Larry, but in Gold Hill he was known exclusively as Bear. His wife was Poppy. Their children were grown; the central object of Poppy's life was a lovely auburn border collie improbably named Morgaine (there was a theme: a predecessor had been named Ygraine, and there was a cat called Merlin), with whom I fell instantly in love when I visited over a long Memorial Day weekend.

Bear and Poppy's house sat on a small rise above Gold Hill Road on the easternmost side of the little grid. It was long and low, with a shallow front porch offering an overview of what was going on in most of the town. The porch opened into a big living room with barn wood walls and a nice fireplace. Behind it was a large kitchen; to the right were the original two bedrooms, now filled with clothes and boxes. Off to the left, a master bedroom had been added as well as a greenhouse, tiled and glass-walled, that doubled as a dining room and looked out into the backyard. The décor was eclectic cabin-shabby with Asian touches—stone Buddhas, carved screens, woven hangings and rugs. I learned that Poppy and Bear had a daughter living in Thailand whom they visited often.

Over the weekend we had dinner at the Gold Hill Inn, a single-story log structure built in 1924 as a dining hall for the westering Bluebirds. Locals Barbara and Frank Finn bought both the inn and the former hotel in 1962 and turned the inn into an upscale restaurant in a happily downscale site; their sons now owned and operated it. We walked into the lobby—a long, dim room featuring stone fireplaces at each end, ancient, unreliable- and inhospitable-looking bentwood furniture, and a bar in the southwest corner. Only a honky-tonk piano playing "Camptown Races" was missing to convince me that I was in *Silverado*. We sidled up to the bar and ordered something to sip while waiting to be called to our table inside. A couple locals were congregated there (as I would learn they habitually were), not planning on dinner, and they checked us out carefully. The dining room was more like a big dining hall: a scattering of tables with checkered cloths, wildflowers in small vases, and a heterogeneous assortment of chairs. We had already placed our order, selecting from a reassuringly limited six-course menu that ran for the whole summer season and a decent wine list. The place was open only a few nights per week, and only through the early fall, when the potbelly stove would be lit. Even locals called for reservations, as the inn was usually packed with people flocking up from Boulder or elsewhere across the Front Range, as I quickly learned to call the eastern side of the Rockies.

As we stepped outside the inn that night to walk the two blocks back to Bear and Poppy's place, I was stopped short by the sky: azure deepening to indigo, riddled with stars. Sheltered from the brightness of the Denver-Boulder corridor, Gold Hill made a kind of shallow bowl-shaped star catcher. Was it that night, or was it later, that we sat in the backyard, faces tilted up, watching the star show play across the blue-black dome that became more crowded as it darkened? Occasionally a transcontinental jet would blink soundlessly, far above, or a comet would streak a brief arc. I reached for Bob's hand in the dark. As always, he quickly surrounded my fingers with his own. His hands were large, muscular, squared off. Capable and safe, and somehow definitive.

✳

When Bob came to Michigan for Christmas 1999, he had been in Colorado for two years. That December I had recently been granted my third sabbatical, so we were eyeing the next year together in Colorado. When the gifts had all been opened and nothing remained under the tree except my new kitten, Scout, who was trying to climb it, I reached for the mysterious envelope lodged in its branches—manila, with a red bow stuck on it and my name written on the front. Inside were sketches, clearly not Bob's, of rings. They looked pseudo-medieval, as if rendered by a Dungeons and Dragons geek. Some, I noticed, incorporated griffins in my honor. And there was a letter, which ended with a question: would I spend the rest of my life with him?

Across the room in a chair, clad in the gray sweats he wore to bed in winter, Bob wept as I read the letter, carried away by his own moment.

And at that moment, I balked. To this day I wonder why. Precisely what step was I unwilling to take, after ten years together? Was it he who made me hesitate or myself, his limitations or my own? Was it because the sporadic nature of our visits hadn't allowed us enough time physically together? A fear of hitching my life to another, of what exactly this would bind me to? The institution of marriage, which I didn't hold in particular esteem?

But was this, after all, a proposal of marriage? The letter hadn't actually included the m-word. Something about the ambiguity seemed appropriate to our brand of togetherness.

Bob was now talking about having met with an artisan about designing a ring for me and finally deciding not to proceed without consulting me. We talked a bit about designs. Finally, after a pause, he said, "You haven't answered my question," and I let it spill from me: "Of course I will."

We would complete the ring project in Boulder, we decided. As we talked about the year to come, I issued what I guess amounted to an ultimatum, though it felt like a simple statement of fact: I want to come to Boulder, but I cannot live and write a book in the Concrete Palace. Not long into the new millennium, when Bob was back in Colorado, one of our phone conversations began this way: "How would you like to live in Gold Hill?" Bear had offered a solution: he too would be on leave next year and he and Poppy were planning to travel; having passed the test of Morgaine-sitting to Poppy's satisfaction, would Bob now consider occupying the Gold Hill house and caring for her for a year?

I couldn't imagine living in that weird Neverland. But on the other hand: no rent, room to live, a cool house, and a great dog. "But hon, the Oldsmobile has to go."

"What?! It's a classic!" Which is what he always said.

We both bought SUVs. Packed to the roof, mine left Michigan in June 2000.

✱

It never took Bob long to settle into a new place. He made his space, poured his martini, and was home. I am a different animal, hypersensitive to my physical environment. I have to work hard to make a place mine. And this was the strangest place I'd ever perched. I had asked Poppy about cell service and she looked confused, turned to Bear, and said, "I don't think anybody's ever gotten a cell signal up here, have they?" We had dial-up Internet, with its burbles and hisses and bleeps that suggested you were calling the moon or another century. We did have a working TV with several channels, so I got Bob hooked on *West Wing*. Usually we had hot water, sometimes not, which made personal ablutions iffy. We adjusted in increments; we grew into the place. One night Bob's friend Ron, now his boss, and his wife, Jan, drove up for dinner at the Gold Hill Inn and found us sitting side by side on the porch, waiting for them. They got out of the car, already laughing. I guess we looked like an Old West version of *American Gothic*.

Our days found their routine. Bob left early to drive "down the hill." I read, wrote, walked Morgaine. Occasionally I was visited by Merlin, Gold Hill's sole cat. In a place where any animal smaller than a big dog was speedily picked off by coyotes or mountain lions, Merlin had somehow beaten the game. A big orange tom, he nominally belonged to Bear and Poppy but spent long periods out and about, appearing at various friendly houses every few weeks to pay respects and see what was on offer, foodwise. Mostly he sheltered across the street from us at the home of Sharon—the arithmetician of the town sign. He was, even beyond most cats, the embodiment of insouciant cool.

At the end of his workday, Bob would generally call to find out if we needed anything before he drove up. When he got home, NPR came on and the gin bottle and martini glass came out of the freezer. When he started dinner prep, there was music.

We came from disparate musical territories. I found my musical awakening with the Beatles. He was born five years earlier, which put him in a different generation, musically speaking. He went through puberty accompanied by Jerry Lee Lewis and early Elvis, but it was doo-wop that really rocked his world. He couldn't listen to the Ink Spots or the Platters without slow-dancing around the room, bobbing and weaving with me or his own reverie. He even managed to lure me into the province of country music, for which I'd cultivated the usual northern/intellectual/upper-middle-class disdain. I probably heard Randy Travis's album *Old 8×10* for the first time on the Oldsmobile's tape player as we sped through the dark hills on the Massachusetts-Vermont border at night. I asked Bob to play one track over and over. It's bobbing, lilting tune and unabashed romance had hooked me: "I want you to know that my love for you / Is written in stone."

The overlap in our musical Venn diagram contained the Stones, Janis Joplin, and especially Bonnie Raitt—white performers with prominent roots in black music. Bob's tape collection included lots of blues and jazz, territory not unknown to me but still foreign. The witty suggestiveness of blues lyrics became part of our private language. After he hauled in armfuls of logs from the stack in the yard, I'd drape my arm over his shoulders. "My wood man is a good man." If I came into the kitchen at a great musical moment, he would turn and whirl me around the room. He loved to dance 1950s style, as he had learned from his big sister, turning me in complicated patterns, under and over, back and forth, one hand or two, reeling me in and spinning me out. "Is you is or is you ain't my baby!" It came out more statement than question, but I always answered.

"I definitely is."

✳

I had to learn to breathe. On my first trip, I had been startled to feel lightheaded even at the Denver airport. By the time we got up to Gold Hill, walking up the gentlest grade was a challenge, and there is no flat plane in or around town. Plus, the world had neglected to inform me that alcohol's effects increase proportionally as oxygen decreases, so I found myself unaccountably smashed on two gin and tonics.

I acclimated fast, because it was on me to walk Morgaine each day. All I had known about border collies was how pretty and alert their faces are. I quickly learned two more significant facts. First, they must walk—and run—daily, for long distances. It's imperative. And second, they are "eye dogs." That is, their herding history predisposes them to study faces for signals. Morgaine was the most patient of dogs, but every time I looked up from the computer, she was watching me. When I rose to get a glass of water or go to the bathroom, the watching went on high alert. This took some time to get used to.

In the early afternoon, I reached a stopping point and asked, "Wanna go?" And then such joy, as if the entire world waited for her, as I guess it did. I generally took her around what locals called the Loop. Sometimes we began by climbing up into the Meadow, a broad hillside of tall grasses and wildflowers, forested on top. It was from those high trees that coyotes yipped and howled some nights. On the Meadow's far side was the cemetery. Some graves from the mining period endured. Some told little tales of great sadness—two parental markers fronting five small stone lozenges roughly carved with single names, one name appearing twice, a baby named for an older sibling gone. A dilapidated wrought-iron fence with a gate surrounded a sunken, time-blackened slab. I had seen much older stones in Massachusetts, and even in the cemetery in the village where I grew up in Michigan. This was the paradox of the West for me: the relatively recent story told in these stones measured against the mountains' saga, told in geologic time. And then too, somewhere in this landscape, far less visible to my eyes, was the story of people who honored their dead in ways other than by carving their names into stone.

Morgaine hurried me back down to the road, where she would trot out in front of me, turn, and drop into position, demanding instructions, shifting weight from one front paw to another like an expectant tennis player, eyes like shiny flint. On my cue—"Yoouuu better *go!*"—she was off, a bullet tearing the air, paws barely skimming the hard road, ears and red coat streaming behind her. It was a thing to see. And the whole routine had to be repeated, all the way home.

Our halfway point was a rocky footpath on the right that led to the top of a high hill. Morgaine clambered happily up; I came laboring after. It became a goal to do the hill without stopping. At the top was a big rock where I sat to recover, while Morgaine waited patiently. I could look out over the Front Range—the sharp top edges of the Flatirons were actually visible—and across the plain far below to the misty spires of Denver. Breezes floated, sweet with grasses and wildflowers. I thought about Bob, in his office or at a meeting, hustling, making friends, making notes, greeting everyone he passed, doing his day. How far away the East felt, with its complexities and histories, and how distant my life there seemed. I saw how easy it is to fall into the delusion that the West is simpler or freer; I understood how white people came to think that way. The landscape seems so vast, the sky so wide, that they swallow your own narrative and drown the uproar of the "real life" that suddenly seems less real. And Bob commuted between these realities every day when he drove down the hill and back up again.

After a few minutes of rumination and deep breathing, we set off through a brief strip of dense forest where we once startled a whole herd of deer. The little path came out on a dirt driveway cutting through the Colorado Ranch property. No one seemed to care that we were there except the horses, who came over to snuffle my hand. I fed them weeds; Morgaine was completely uninterested in them. The ranch fronted on Gold Hill Road, where we turned right and headed—blessedly downward—into town. We both slurped water and panted and sat on the porch for a while, looking over the roofs and backyards of the town and listening to the day.

✳

There is not much red or orange in a Colorado autumn, but there is gold in those hills. The sky seems to get bluer as the aspens leave their silvery green behind. Early that fall I happened to read that the largest stand of aspen in the world is in the Gunnison River valley in Colorado. A stand of aspen looks like thousands of trees, but in fact it is a single root system, of which the individual trees are simply varied expressions.

So one shining October weekend we drove west to the Gunnison. Now, there are only a few zillion acres of aspen in proximity to the river, so I'm not sure how I thought we were going to find that one record-breaking stand. Perhaps I just wanted to wander around near it. If Bob thought our quest was an exercise in absurdity, he never said so. We drove around fairly aimlessly until at one point, coming up out of Crested Butte, we found ourselves looking down a long valley toward a snowy peak. From a point high up on the left, a wide, brilliant wave of gold poured down the hill and up the other side. Miles and miles of it against the dark firs and purpled mountains under that electric blue Colorado sky. All one being, one life.

I have a picture of Bob standing in front of it.

✷

We absorbed the local lore and learned the names of distinctive characters. Bear was not the only one with a Gold Hill identity; one longtime resident with a long, snowy beard was known universally only as Prospector. Whoever else he had once been had been left behind down on the plains. Everyone had a story about Twinkle, the town mule, who wandered from house to house all day. Recommended by Bear and Poppy, we were seconded by Sharon Conlin, our neighbor across the street, a wise and witty psychotherapist who also turned out to be the trickster responsible for turning the town sign into an arithmetic problem. There may have been weed involved. Anyway, we were accepted into Gold Hill society and became part of a small group that often convened for dinner or drinks. The women were artists or therapists or both, often affiliated with Naropa University, where Allen Ginsberg founded his Jack Kerouac School of Disembodied Poetics. Many of the men were scientists, retired or otherwise. Nearly everybody skied and kayaked and snowshoed and rafted the white water, and they were all thin and muscled and leathery-skinned. Bob and I, both round and given mostly to indoor pursuits, were distinct anomalies. As such we were objects of fascination, too. When Bob took his job, the local paper ran a story calling him CU's Alcohol Czar. Bear confessed that for the first year of their acquaintance he suspected that Bob might be a narc insinuating himself among the residents of Gold Hill. Given the quality of the locally grown, very pure weed that was always in ample supply at dinners and parties, they had reason to worry. Bob, constitutionally conservative as he was, stuck to his martinis. I availed myself of all that was on offer. Word would go around that there was a party at, say, John and Cherry's the following night. Everyone would show up with their dogs and some wine and food to contribute; we got good and loaded, ate very well, and waddled home under the stars.

Sometimes these gatherings, with no change in personnel, took the guise of the Gold Hill Literary Society. Or rather, one of them: there was also one that met monthly around the woodstove down at the store. This was the other one, and its rules were fairly lenient. You could bring something original, or you could bring a passage of some book you were enjoying. Or you could bring nothing. Your original could be new, or it might be something everyone had heard six years ago. Everyone had all been friends for years—raised children together, seen each other through divorces and deaths, traveled together, and come home again to this town, this little joke on the world. Frankly, we felt honored to be included.

Periodically, to great and excited heraldry, Jack and Linda appeared. Their cabin was on the lower reaches of Horsfal, but they were usually elsewhere, in their California desert home or tooling around the country in their shiny 1950s silver Airstream. When they returned to Gold Hill, a party always materialized, generally at their place. Linda was like a little bird, quick and vocal. Jack was a very tall man of few words, a John Huston type, a retired engineer and a great storyteller, careful and slow. There were always stories at Gold Hill gatherings: tales of fires, snowstorms, extramarital affairs, accidents, characters done and gone. One night Jack told this one, well known to everyone but Bob and me.

On a November night in 1972, a few days after a big snow, he was driving home from work along the Shelf Road when he saw in the beam from his headlights a small figure in the road, waving him down. It was a young girl. She was not wearing winter gear, and from one of her wrists dangled what he soon was able to identify as a handcuff. He got her into the truck, wrapped her in his coat, and headed toward town. Her name was Annabelle. She told him that a man had kidnapped her and her girlfriend off the street in Boulder and taken them to his motor home, where he handcuffed them together. Then he had driven them—and his dog—up here, forced the girls out onto the side of the road, and shot them. The impact of the shots sent them over the edge of the Shelf. Annabelle thought her friend was dead, but she herself had been only slightly wounded. She had managed to pull her friend's hand out of the cuff and climb through the snow up the cliff to the road. Would he take her home to Boulder?

Two details would emerge later: before bringing them up here, their abductor had sexually assaulted the girls. And it was Annabelle's eleventh birthday.

Jack looked at the wound in her leg. The bleeding was slight, probably slowed by the cold. So he continued into town. Remembering that a volunteer fire department meeting was taking place at a neighbor's house, he stopped and carried Annabelle inside. The volunteer firemen administered first aid and called the Boulder sheriff's department.

But Jack wasn't done yet: what if Annabelle's friend was still alive? He went home, put on heavy boots, loaded his pistol, and he and two guys from the fire department headed back up the Shelf Road. They found the imprints in the snow of the man, his dog, and the two girls. Jack shone his flashlight down the cliffside. The beam found a small body, face-up in the snow. They scaled down what Jack estimated to be a forty-degree incline in the dark, in deep snow, and checked for vital signs. There were none. The trio climbed up and headed back to town.

Back at the fire department meeting Annabelle, not yet finished amazing everyone, was able to give the sheriff's department not only a full description of the abductor and his motor home but also the license number. To be fair, a description of the captor would not have been difficult: he was dressed in green tights, a skirt, a poncho, and a woman's hat. He was intercepted in Sunshine Canyon within the hour, by which time Annabelle was at Boulder Hospital.

From that night on, whenever I came onto the Shelf Road on the way home, I always saw a half-frozen little wraith in the road, waving a handcuffed arm. And a tall man easing himself over the edge, where I was afraid even to look.

✳

It's odd, what moments stick in memory.

One clear night in early winter, an inch or so of snow on the ground, I took Morgaine for an extra walk, a short jaunt northwest of town, up the private driveway of the woman who was heir to the Laura Ashley textile fortune. "No Trespassing" signs were clearly posted, but I had been encouraged to ignore them by the locals. I don't think we went all the way up the long two-track drive to the manse itself—a colossal three-story log home on steroids. We just went up a ways and turned around. But before we headed home, we walked a little into a grove of trees at the bottom of the driveway. Further on was a small constellation of trailers that looked mostly empty. I stopped and looked up. The sun had just set and darkness was closing in fast, but there was light in the sky, some pink and cantaloupe-colored streaks in the clouds. A bright moon shone. Everything was very silent, and it was cold but not bitter. I breathed, and I seemed to experience that simple act profoundly. I was attuned to each inhalation, and I watched each exhalation materialize and then dissipate in the dusky air. To one side, dark evergreen forest and a steep drop into Left Hand Canyon; to the other, just yards away from this spot, the warmly lit windows of town. Two Gold Hill blocks away, Bob was making dinner.

I stood there in that moment for a while, taking in the cold, clean air, feeling the night come. *Here I am.* Strange, and lovely.

Morgaine studied me quizzically. "Okay," I told her, "let's go." She trotted off through the snow, and I followed.

✳

Later in winter we hit our impasse, Bob and I, like a car running into a fresh snowdrift—a silent, nonviolent, complete stop. I wonder what it says about me or about him, or maybe just about partnership, that the safety I felt with him could so easily be blown out the window, as if a stiff north wind had suddenly swept through. He would withdraw, distant and unresponsive, leaving me feeling abandoned and alone. He had lived solo for many years, even during his previous marriage, and here I was, wanting connection and warmth. But somewhere in his life he had learned to go inside himself and shut the door. It was probably self-protective but sometimes, when he didn't want to deal with me or was put off by something I'd done, it was punitive. Always it felt like being locked outdoors.

I was angry that when this happened Bob could go on obliviously while I could think of nothing else but how our common life was guttering. One night, having resorted to the couch in misery, I lay staring up at the ceiling. I couldn't imagine how he could sleep in our big bed without me, without making things all right, knowing how unhappy I was. I couldn't imagine how he could push me away when I had driven eleven hundred miles and committed a year of my life to being here, to being with him. I felt exposed, endangered, isolated—and stranded. *I have to get out of here,* I thought. I found myself making an escape plan. I would go back to Kalamazoo, but where would I live? My house was rented for the year. Maybe my sisterfriend Diane would let me occupy her upper story, which she never used. Maybe I could rent an apartment. Maybe the college had a vacant house. Unable to live in this terrible chill, I was hurrying to shut my doors and windows, reestablish my boundaries, get myself safe.

When I was an adolescent and thought my mother didn't understand me or had treated me unjustly, I resorted to writing her letters, which I would leave on her pillow. Sometimes she wrote me back. In extremity I still never quite trust my speaking voice; I have to write. And so I did: the next morning I drafted a long email to Bob. I think it had the classic three parts—here's what's happened; here's how it makes me feel; and here's what needs to happen next—and I was quite specific about the third part: we seek counseling, or I have to leave.

And like that, the ice dam broke loose. Bob acted as if he'd woken up and realized he'd overslept. In response to my grand opera, he was reasonable, gentle, generous, practical. The sheer difference in size of our responses was embarrassing, even though I've heard for most of my life that I tend toward dramatic hyperbole. It was something I had to learn repeatedly with Bob, and maybe the most important thing I learned—that conflict did not spell disaster; that he would not walk away and could be trusted with what I actually felt. There was also the lesson about myself: I had customarily thought of myself as dangerously capable of losing myself in anything that might pass as love. As it turned out, I wasn't. With minimal time or struggle I knew that rather than be this lonely with Bob, I would seek to be alone. When I needed myself, there I was. On the couch that night, my ability to plan felt like sanctuary, like solace. Possibly Bob's withdrawal inside himself, which read as cold and unloving to me, provided the same for him.

This was not the last time we hit this very impasse. That came eight years later, a couple months before his death, at our Michigan cabin. Weeping, I had my epiphany: "This is the same fucking fight we're going to have for the rest of our lives, isn't it?"

We both started to laugh. I continued. "And I will always be the one to have to say something about it, won't I?"

He sighed. "Probably you will, hon. Because I just won't see it coming."

I resented having to play Relationship Custodian, one of the more exhausting traditionally female roles. I wondered how a man could learn to observe human dynamics as acutely as Bob did, probably through his professional training, and not put the same skills to work at home. But I remember also feeling, as we started to laugh, the profound calm of knowing that a big, long love includes your trademark fight. It was, weirdly, a comfortably known quantity. I would have to continue to make us struggle. But I would no longer fear the apocalypse or plan an escape. But in Gold Hill, the struggle was new and still frightening. So we did a fairly short stint with a couples therapist in Boulder who made clear, without saying so outright, that we were way, way down near the bottom of the scale of couples at risk.

It seems so obvious and natural to me now; of course we struggled, coming together as we did: two humans no longer young and long accustomed to living on our own terms, in our own modes, by our own rhythms, in a relationship mostly characterized by arrivals and departures and temporary intimacies.

That winter we also made friends with the eternal presence of the dominant parents sharing our common life. Bud would always be there, going at life as if it were an adversary, measuring his son according to an unchangeable Man template, demanding to know the plan for the beans. My formidable mother would also always be with us, and when I got particularly invested in having things done my way, Bob took to quietly responding, "Yes, Barbara." Our other ghost parents were around too: Bob's lovely, talented, alcoholic mother; my cold, critical father, who probably haunted me in Bob's form throughout that night I spent on the sofa.

I came to look forward to our counseling appointments, which we always followed with a great lunch out. It became my favorite day of the week, sort of like date night. Bob started to brag about our therapy in social situations, to the confusion of plenty of people. And as spring came, we moved ahead with the notion of having rings designed. Among the populous artisan community of Boulder, we found a jewelry artist we liked and commissioned him to make two circles of white gold featuring an inlaid rectangle of polished agate. We never said we were engaged, never even discussed the rings' meaning because we knew it: we were together.

✳

Gold Hill had its own weather, which usually bore no resemblance to whatever was happening down in Boulder. On a dark, snowy-wet forty-five-degree day I would drive down the hill and find myself in a city shimmering in sixty-five-degree sunshine under a searing blue sky, where the students had broken out their surfer shorts and skateboards. Sometimes a whitish miasma would slide quietly into town, blanking out everything. It was something I'd never seen before—not fog, not frost. It actually coated the branches of trees, and when I touched it, I found it weirdly sticky. Then one day I read that the cloud cover over Boulder was at approximately eight thousand feet, and I realized that we were literally living in the clouds. Cloud matter swathed our house and painted the aspen branches. It seemed to enter my head too, depressing me and making me feel captive and isolated and yearning for the flatlands.

The snow, too, was radically different from what I'd known all my life: bone-dry, squeaking like Styrofoam underfoot, impossible to compact into a ball. Winter wasn't the Overlook Hotel snow-pocalypse I'd imagined. As a rule, it's the places that don't expect it that are immobilized by snow. The more snow a place gets, the better its equipment will be. In the Rocky Mountains, snow is removed by full-scale bulldozers that essentially regrade the dirt roads as they push through. Getting to the road from our cabin and back again was another matter, requiring major shoveling, which Bob always did at an alarming pace—his log-splitting pace, the pace of a man who saw his work as an opponent to fight into submission. The big drifts glorified the town. At the end of a walk Morgaine would snowplow nose-first through the long snowbank in front of the house in utter ecstasy.

Spring in the Rockies is another thing altogether. At first I thought it came early, as some brilliant sun began to melt the snow in early March. I soon came to realize that a mountain spring means wild vacillation. There were seventy-degree walks with Morgaine and no jacket; there were blizzards; there was ice.

In May I finished a draft of the book I was working on, and I set my departure for the 15th of June. Bear and Poppy returned to their Boulder house, and I delivered Morgaine and said good-bye. On the 14th, we had a wet, heavy blizzard.

Bob always said good-bye as if he would see me in a matter of days. "Call tonight?" he said, kissing me as he left for work the next morning. When I got down to Boulder it was brilliantly sunny. I have no idea how I got lost on the way out of a city I had been navigating for a year. It took me a full hour to leave Boulder behind and head east across the plains, back home, back to work, back to the world where planes were about to fly into towers, ushering in a new millennium.

✳

Bear and Poppy wanted their house back, so Bob faced homelessness. But he had Gold Hill bona fides now, so Jack and Linda invited him to move into their place in exchange for a little rent and maintenance work during their long absences. Thus was he able to stay in Gold Hill for the six more years he would be at CU. He came to Michigan for most Christmases, rooted there by family as well as by me. One year he was preceded by a rectangular parcel about two feet by one and a half, maybe two inches thick, and remarkably heavy. Inside was a slab of rosy granite inscribed, IT'S WRITTEN IN STONE.

"You should have seen the guy who engraved it, trying to figure out what I wanted to say," Bob said. "I kept saying, 'It's written in stone!' and he kept looking at me. 'Crazy flatlander. Probably from the university.'"

I visited him many times. One memorable spring break I arrived at the tail end of a blizzard that kept me in Boulder overnight before the roads opened sufficiently to allow Bear, who'd been stranded in town as well, to ferry me up to Gold Hill. But none of the driveways had been cleared and I had to climb up to Jack and Linda's cabin through thigh-high drifts. Two local kids kindly portered my suitcase. The snow was up above the cabin's back windows, making it very dark inside, and periodically Bob had to shovel the roof.

But my visits were usually in summer. I spent long, bright, dry days writing out in Jack's little log studio or reading in the one easy chair Bob owned. Like most Gold Hill cabins, this one had an addition, a long room ending in a big dining table and a lovely bay window looking out over the hill and down to the road on its way out of town and the Meadow beyond it. One day, sitting there, I looked up to meet the eyes of what was either a bobcat or a lynx about ten feet away, making its way up the hill. The cabin porch looked down over the town, and Long's Peak was visible in the far distance on clear days, when there was a great gold-and-pink sunset over the Divide. One night after we'd come home from Boulder and Bob had fallen into bed, I sat out there in the cool dark blue air. A full moon was rising over Horsfal, directly behind the cabin. As the light increased and the shadows before me intensified, its imminence was palpable, as if it were a huge living power coming up behind me. I made myself stay, almost frightened.

✳

At the end of summer 2007, after ten years in Boulder, Bob retired. We didn't ever really discuss his next move; it was somehow implicit that he would return to Michigan. I was heading into my fourth and final sabbatical, during which Bob and I would make it legal. In August I drove west one last time. At farewell events at the university he was given cards with dozens of signatures, toasts celebrating his achievements, photo montages, and polished granite versions of Ralphie the Buffalo, the university's mascot. We spent a few days packing up and cleaning out, and by "we" I mean "I," as he was still going to work. I plundered the hoard of near-empty boxes Bob had been moving around the country for several decades, consolidated their contents, and broke them all down for the recycling run. When he came home at 5:30, he found me filthy, T-shirt clinging to my body, hair plastered to my head, and he wasn't nearly grateful enough.

Bob's lush rosemary plant, so helpful for pork roasts, went fully buffered onto the floor of the back seat of my car, and one September morning our two laden vehicles pulled out of town over the Shelf Road. In my rearview mirror as we skirted Horsfal, a girl wavered in the middle of the road, having crawled from death back up into her life. With her unshackled wrist, she was waving.

✳

Eight months later, when Bob died, the Gold Hill gang all called or wrote in shock and grief. After that, contact was sporadic. Sharon called occasionally to check on me and report wryly that she thought of Bob every time she used the compost bin he'd bequeathed to her when he left. In 2010 a monster fire roared up Four-Mile Canyon, burning over six thousand acres and destroying 160 dwellings, but the town itself survived yet again. Sometime after there came an email from Poppy to a world of people, announcing that Morgaine had died. *The best dog in the world*, she wrote. And in 2012, Annabelle returned to Gold Hill. Jack and Linda organized a reunion of the folks who had saved her life that night forty years earlier, after she had saved her own. Annabelle said she wanted to say thank you, and to show everyone she'd turned out all right, her life had gone on. She was married now, a mother.

When I fled the cabin on the Manistee two days after Bob died, I somehow managed to take the rosemary plant with me. But in Kalamazoo I neglected it and one day it was entirely brown. Rosemary, for remembrance.

✳

A couple nights before we left Gold Hill, Poppy and Bear hosted a farewell feast at their house. It was like most late summer/early fall nights there: clear, cool, full of stars. Bob—having been required, even as guest of honor, to mix the martinis, in deference to his expertise—drank them steadily. I did my gin and tonics, my wine with dinner, and my share of the fierce mountain weed—which is to say maybe two hits, more than enough. We hugged and thanked everyone and then the two of us began to stagger home.

We moved through the silent streets. The dark inn, the closed-up store, the funny old cabins, familiar but still strange by night. The abandoned red pickup that had sat in the grass above Pine Street for decades. A huge moon cast our shadows on the hard-packed, rutted main drag. We held onto each other, laughing. I stopped once to look up, stumbling slightly. "Look," I said. "We won't see these stars again."

When Bob gazed up, he began to topple, so I grabbed his arm and we walked on.

I go back to that moment and implore everything to stop there. I beg those wheeling stars to spin us up and dissolve us into their vortex. But they were wheeling, after all. So we kept moving too, through the empty streets of that improbable place, two unlikely, drunken lovers beneath the fervent moon, eternally working their way home.

GRIEF'S COUNTRY

After the night of the open door, a morning comes, outrageously. It is brilliant and clear, a perfect May day. I am alone, standing in the living room of the cabin, looking out the dining room window, unseeing, waiting to move.

I am paralyzed in contradiction. It is impossible that this has happened, yet I know this has happened. But the spiking images cannot be real—they are too outlandish. So I am stuck, unable to move in the world of time.

We have been married four months and eight days, so this cannot have happened. It cannot have happened here, at our cabin, our stake in a joint future. It cannot have happened when he only went outside to bring the bird feeders in, as he did every night, to keep them from raccoons. It cannot be that he never came back. That makes no sense. But I feel twigs and mud in my matted hair, so my memory of sliding down into the river to find him must be true. An image lurks at the edge of my mind: slippers, one under the big white pine, one on the lower bank, inches from the water. I could not have imagined such a thing so it must have happened. And he must be gone, because I am here alone.

I have been alone all night. The police and neighbors were gone by 1 a.m. After asking me repeatedly if I would be all right, they left me, so I must have said I would be. Of course I did. I made five mandatory, dreadful phone calls, to his two siblings and two children and to Diane. I took a call from a stranger, a mortician, and said *cremation*.

I don't know how I did this, disembodied as I was, as I am. Some part of me seems to be functioning as a kind of emissary from the unavailable remainder of myself. Maybe the deepest part of me after all is my incorrigible sense of responsibility. Or maybe that part kicks in as an attempt to throw some kind of anchor into reality lest I float entirely away. The way I grabbed that branch in the river.

After the calls I lay on our bed, trying to breathe, staving off the recognition that he would never lie here next to me again. My hair was still damp. My body was adrenalin-scoured, shaky and nauseated. Time fractured and folded back on itself, sending me periodically back into the river, screaming. I slept in ragged fragments, jerking awake and yelling. I tried to quiet and calm myself viscerally, as if I were a traumatized animal in my own care.

Now, on this brilliant morning in May, I find myself Elsewhere —still in human life, apparently, but in a province unknown and fearsome. The place I have come from, the one where I have a life with Bob, is gone, and if I allow myself to think about it for longer than a millisecond I will shatter on the floor. This new place is uninhabitable but must be inhabited.

I am fifty-seven. I have lost many people, including four parents. I don't have to be convinced, as young grievers do, that the pain will lessen, that the monstrous event will slowly seep into my life like chemicals seeping into groundwater. I know this will happen, and that's the problem: the prospect of how much time must be lived through in order for that process to occur is more than I can think about. First I will have to bring myself to believe in last night. The time it will all take stretches before me like a wasteland. I want to opt out, yield to disaster, collapse in the face of it and die. I want to be put away somewhere safe until I am fit to live.

But standing here in the middle of the cabin, staring around me, trying to understand that this nightmare is real, I am, in fact, already living through it. *You are living right now,* I remind myself. So I might as well move, one foot and then another, toward the shower, to wash the river out of my hair. And then, breathing shallowly, get dressed. And then actually blow-dry my hair, as if it mattered. And then, moving very slowly but methodically, wash the dishes from the dinner we ate together last night, without thinking of the dinner we ate together last night. They will just be dishes, soaking in now-cold water where he put them last night. How they got there I will not think about. I take off my grandmother's wedding ring so it doesn't go down the drain. I don't put it on again.

And it goes from there, step after step toward noon, when people begin to show up and I am held, and decisions are made, and the earth begins to turn.

✳

Somehow it has been arranged that Linda, the widow of a stepbrother, will take custody of me. She lives an hour away on the Lake Michigan shore. She takes me to an emergency care center where a kind, gentle P.A. checks me out. She also takes me to the funeral home in Kalkaska, the one that called me in the middle of the night. She knows things like how many copies of a death certificate one needs. At her house I watch the lake, which brings moments of something like calm.

Three days later I am ferried downstate to my house in Kalamazoo. Entering my house, I walk into immediate and unexpected relief, a sense of safety and comfort. I am no longer in the Terrible Place, our poor little cabin, poisoned like a well with a body in it. I never want to see it again. Here, I can breathe a little. Diane shows up on my porch. Later she tells me that when she put her arms around me I wasn't there in my body.

Two days later my brother and niece arrive from Oregon. He takes over. A lawyer, he pages through Bob's files, pulling documents I will need, writing me instructions, making calls. He also shops and cooks substantial meals that encourage me to eat. He takes care. I vaguely recognize a watershed: my brother and I have been semi-estranged for a long time, reconnecting only recently.

But that was before. This is after, where perspective operates differently. Many enormities have instantly shrunk to insignificance. My niece, sixteen, controls and interprets the television for me and buys me waterproof mascara for a memorial service, organized by Bob's kids, which I can barely bring myself to attend. The two of them shepherd me past displays of photos of Bob that I steadfastly refuse to see, through waves of music that is not Bonnie Raitt or Koko Taylor, not his music.

The summer comes on, with its long bright days to be lived through. Mornings are worst. Birds wake me early, when it's still cool, and a few weightless seconds pass before I remember and sink into my life. Craving unconsciousness, I dive for sleep again as the heat rises.

I tiptoe around my own mind. If I stumble, I will land at the river's edge in the dark, screaming. A too-quick move and I will feel the monstrous fall upon me like an axe. A clumsy turn will bring me face-to-face with Bob's absence, with the incredible fact that I will never see his face again. My head is a dark cave resonating with an endless shriek.

Reading is the sole activity that keeps it all at bay, so I read the hours away. Gradually I take on one minor task per day, like dishwashing or laundry. When I can accomplish two things, I congratulate myself. Like a person recovering from a debilitating illness, I feel my limits. If it seems too much to walk from one room to another, I don't. Each day is like a closed room. Looking back or forward exhausts and terrifies me. So I am here, now, and nowhere else. I am abstracted from the ongoing narrative that constituted myself. It went over the edge, into the river.

Periodically I must confirm to myself that what happened was real. This has nothing to do with denial. It is the difficulty of integrating the unimaginable—not just the terrible but the weird. Realization—making something real—turns out to be a process. I am impatient to get this monstrosity ingested, to swallow the surreal lump and get on with grieving. Like Emily Dickinson, I know I can wade grief, whole pools of it. But this—this is a different beast, a three-headed Cerberus. This bottomless, roiling pain comes flanked by trauma's residual terror on one side and existential outrage on the other. And all three of them howling.

At the very western edge of the eastern time zone the summer sun hangs in the sky, glaring, invasive, until after 8:30, when the light begins to thin. Finally, by 9:30, night starts to bloom up from the earth and drown the sky, which is still bright in the west an hour later. I breathe in the cool, the dark reprieve. I welcome the television voices, or read some more. Another day lived through.

Several years after all this, two thousand miles from home, I will see a dog lying on a sidewalk, his person kneeling beside him. The dog isn't dead or even bleeding, but it has been *stricken*. People stop to offer help, but the human just kneels and waits. It is as if he knows the dog is waiting too, to see if its life returns.

✳

When I arrive home in Kalamazoo, five days after Bob's death, I immediately notice that the house and yard are pristine. Friends from the college have had the place professionally cleaned; a crew of them has mowed my grass, blown clean my walkways, and raked my gardens. Part of the huge relief I feel upon walking into the house is the calm of order and cleanliness. Neither my friends nor I could have known how important this would be.

Diane has coordinated everything, functioning as Information Central for the world of people concerned about me. She turns her attention to me like a doctor making rounds. At first she calls thrice daily—morning, afternoon, night—to gauge my state of being. One day when she asks how I am I hear myself wail, "I'm mad at Bob!"

"Why?"

"He wasn't supposed to leave me!"

This is where I start to laugh, and she joins in. It's the first time I've laughed. It's a bit like a dam breaking. As I become increasingly functional, the calls diminish to two a day. By the end of June, it's one.

My friend Karyn is the nexus of the food network that has been organized—scheduling, collecting meals, dropping them off. I am apparently not to be disturbed. I'm grateful for this, but also a little embarrassed. Round about 5:00 in the glaring afternoons through June, after I have inched through the terrible hours, Karyn creeps up to my back door and deposits a container, then creeps away. I'm Bertha Rochester, voiceless, outraged, helpless, fed intermittently by the silent Grace Poole.

Other friends confront my calamity in their own idiom. Chris, for instance, ignores the food network and its vinyl containers of comfort food. He shows up in person, his long, tall figure striding up to my back door wearing shorts, a flowered shirt, and an antique turquoise necklace that I have coveted for years, bearing before him a silver platter featuring charcuterie, an assortment of cheeses, sliced and fanned out, and fresh asparagus, steamed to a brilliant green, chilled, the stalks lined up like soldiers. He wants to plant a tree for Bob. I just want to sink my teeth into the perfect asparagus. I can't tell him, or explain to myself, how comforting it is to have a man with me.

✳

My house is the only safety; it feels like a cave of comfort and protection from a random and terrifying world. I go outside into the yard to see what summer has brought up, but I stay close. My first foray beyond the perimeter comes when Marigene and Mary take me to dinner at a restaurant forty minutes away—chosen, I suspect, so that I won't have to worry about seeing people I know. It feels strange to be out, and the world looks dreamlike, far too bright. I get through dinner and am relieved to reach home again.

Part of my agoraphobia is that when I am around people, I feel my distance from the human species much more acutely than when I'm alone. A recurring mental image: I am standing on an unpopulated shore as a giant ship sails away, bearing a noisy crowd that includes everyone I know and everyone else besides. I am left behind because I have experienced something so far beyond the pale that no one can speak to me or comprehend the words I might find. I desperately want to escape the island, but I can't bear the thought of being onboard that teeming ship where I will be a shadow.

I think of all those people contemplating me, the wreck of me, and I know that they feel nothing but love, sorrow, and pity. But what I feel is shame. Now I know why shame follows trauma. To be truly violated—in your body, in your life—is to be seen and known as completely vulnerable, akin to being naked in public. You become the "carrier," bearing the curse of human powerlessness, the stigma of disaster and delusion. Everything I am has been subsumed by catastrophe, like a sinkhole. After all I have been in my years, I am now only one thing: the person to whom *this* happened.

✳

I do not ask why. I know there is no reason for what's happened. I've always been very clear about the meanings in my life—my work, my writing, my relationships; now Bob's death draws meaninglessness down like a raptor. But sure as I am that the cosmos has shown its utterly indifferent face once and for all, I can't seem to root myself there. I abandoned any notion of a personal deity in high school, yet my mind is constantly running up against God, another name for "Why."

A couple of good friends coincidentally light on the word *cruel* to describe what has befallen me. The word falls into place with a satisfying click, apt and right. I have been the object of a cruel hoax, like Carrie at the prom, and I've now suffered my baptism of blood and I want to explode everything in sight. Like Carrie, I've been led down the garden path. Throughout our eighteen years together I have been writing Bob into the story as redeemer of my isolated life, the late love come to rescue me from my persistent loneness. I, who have preached to generations of students against the deceptions of the Romance Plot; I, who have enjoined young women not to imagine that a man will redeem their lives—I have fallen for the same ruse. The Cosmic Pedagogue has just inter-vened brutally, not merely to demonstrate power but to show me my mistake.

But now we're back to Divine Purpose. What is this version but another narrative, another word-net cast into immensity, no more reliable than romance? While we may have an interest in learning, the universe itself has no interest in teaching us, and no capacity for cruelty, which by definition is intentional.

Which is worse: cruelty or indifference? Something taking aim at me, or a stray bullet finding my heart?

The stories we fashion for our experience constitute a kind of gravity. I bounce between these two incompatible notions like a loose astronaut pinballing between two planets. And neither one can sustain life.

✳

Mary Ellen comes by regularly, to sit quietly with me and check my spiritual vitals. She is chaplain at the college and she per-formed our marriage. Four months later, it was she and her part-ner, Suzanne, who drove north to bring me home. One day she arrives lugging a large, cumbersome black garbage bag she can barely lift. Out tumbles a huge afghan, an accretion of rectangles without pattern or plan: wildly disparate colors, thicknesses, tex-tures, some pieces adorned with beads or pearls or fringe or bits of wood. The pieces have been knitted by various staff and faculty members who answered Mary Ellen's call. The gift comes with a handbook of homemade paper, each page bearing a scrap of yarn and a message from the knitter.

Taking the ungainly softness onto my lap like some big sweet animal, I weep. I cry all the time, but this is the first time I have wept from something other than grief laced with rage. And I'm aware of the change.

Diane mentions that she's about to take her cairn terrier, Doon, to the groomer. I hear myself say, "I want to take her." She demurs; I insist. I want to pay for it too, and Di, with her sensitivity to people's odd needs, accepts. This is the first voluntary car trip I've taken. Doon and I are particular friends, as she affirms by peeing on the kitchen floor whenever I show up. There is something deeply reassuring about ferrying her to the beauty shop and then retrieving her and returning her home—silky and trimmed and clean-smelling, no perfume, no bows. I have done a thing, simple and singular, and the result is good. Doon's matted blond fur has been solved.

✷

People hold death at bay with verbal formulas. No one I know, thankfully, has the *cojones* to tell me that everything happens for a reason, or that God doesn't give us more than we can bear. But one religious friend suggests that possibly Bob's death was a benevolent alternative to paraplegia or some equally horrible outcome of his fall from the riverbank. Because this friend's heart is good, and because we are dining in public, I keep my Medusa mask folded in my purse and simply ask, quietly, why the benevolent alternative couldn't be Bob's *not falling from the bank at all.*

I discover that there is a universal solvent people reach for in the presence of someone coated in death: *Sorry for your loss.* Not even a complete sentence, subject and verb both excised. Shorthand, like a text. *Sry 4 yr ls.* Oftener than not the four words are rushed together. *Sorry fyaloss.* Hearing it is like hearing silence, or worse, depending on who says it.

Many of the cards I receive employ some variant of *You'll always have your memories.* If each of these cards produces a paper cut, I will bleed to death. As I read them—just weeks after Bob was the living, log-splitting, martini-drinking, pork-loin-with-rosemary-cooking, dancing, snoring center point of my life—memory itself is a beast I have to manage assiduously, minute to minute. Memory threatens to rise up and eat me alive. By midafternoon of the day after Bob's death, his brother, at my direction, is hauling out all of Bob's clothes, to be donated or dumped immediately. I see the alarm in his eyes and realize I might seem deranged at best, heartless at worst. But I know that if I see or touch or smell Bob's things hanging in the closet, I will collapse. Who proposed this notion that memories offer any kind of compensation or solace?

With the language of grief on my mind, I find myself fascinated by the messages to dead loved ones printed at the end of the obituaries in the local paper. *It's been ten years and we miss you every day. We know you are in the stars, watching over us. Love, Mom, Dad, Brittany, Mark, Nana, and Pops.* Or: *Happy Birthday, Tom! This would be your 40th.* Faced as I am every waking minute with the conundrum of my beloved man's absence, I am greatly tolerant of all the ways grievers manage their loss. But I have to wonder whether people actually imagine an afterlife where the departed is reading the newspaper. Or celebrating his birthday? Do they regard the *Kalamazoo Gazette* as a portal to the Beyond?

The only thing possibly more ludicrous is a person with a PhD consulting a psychic. I, who believe in no deity and no afterlife, join the company of Mary Todd Lincoln and many others of the Victorian sisterhood. The psychic comes well recommended by one of the smartest, wisest people I know. She costs $125. She immediately tells me that Bob died of a heart attack on the bank before he hit the water.

"But he'd just had his heart monitored and the doctor said it was perfect!"

Heart attack, she insists. "Happens all the time. My daughter works in the cardiac care unit at the hospital, sees it all the time. Oh, wait, I've got him! He's right here."

She means Bob.

"Yes, he says it was a heart attack. He says, 'I know this isn't the way we wanted it, but this is the way it is.'"

And a sob blooms in my throat, because that sounds exactly like something he'd say.

✳

July 1: I am at my desk, sitting before a computer screen. It is the last place I want to be.

Back in May, I was writing a book. In fact, I was nearing its end. It was an anatomy of a student murder-suicide that occurred at Kalamazoo College in 1999. It would have eleven chapters and a brief conclusion, and at the end of April I had finished drafting chapter 9. I usually write quickly, and keeping up my pace of a chapter per month, I planned on finishing a complete draft in June and July. I would take August to recover before returning to the classroom in September.

My inability to contemplate futurity has had a single exception: the only thing I can imagine that could worsen my present situation would be failing to complete this book. In that case, there really would be no reason to persist in breathing, nothing solid to grasp in the oceanic chaos. With two-plus chapters to go, I will need two months at least. And that means I must resume writing in July.

So the day before my fifty-eighth birthday finds me here, confronting the screen. I study the outline. I get out the index cards and lay them in order around the desk. I reread some of chapter 9, just to hear my own voice again, to reacclimate to the world I was creating in that other life, on the far side of the great divide. And then I start to select letters, to hit keys, to write about the impact of a horrific act of violence on a little academic community.

That first day I delete most of what I write. It feels like I'm working in a second language, one in which I've taken only the introductory class. It feels like I've been left with a vocabulary of about two hundred words. *Just keep going. One word after another. Bird by fucking bird, as Anne Lamott says. Just keep making words.*

✳

I have always been drawn to the skeletal figures associated with the Day of the Dead. Something about their insouciance, their irony, appeals to me strongly. In the hideous ironies clamping down on my life now I sometimes hear rasping laughter—not my own but something laughing at me, or deep in me. The skeleton's grin makes awful sense to me, the cackle at the far end of the scream.

One beastly afternoon when I am capable of leaving the house alone for longer than a few minutes, I head to the multiplex to see *The Dark Knight*. There, leering down at me through grimy grease-paint, is the strangest angel I could have been sent. His power is so unsettling that no one can look away that summer, least of all me. Heath Ledger, dead just this past January, has left a stunning avatar: a shattered, grimy visage, so ugly it is spectacularly beautiful. The traditional Joker makeup has melted into a smeared, sneering parody of itself. The totemic grin is not drawn onto the face but carved—which becomes a grim joke in itself as the Joker offers several different accounts of how it happened, each horrible, each undercutting the previous explanation. The swiping, obscene lizard tongue, the eyes rolling back, the flat, nasal midwestern voice quavering with a disturbing excitement. It only heightens the effect to recall periodically throughout the film that I am watching a dead man perform.

Alone with him in the air-conditioned dark, I am ravished. He is the face of my calamity, of whatever spirit presides over the world I now inhabit. He is the first thing the world has offered that has satisfied me, the first that embodies the noxious stew roiling in me. A brilliant hybrid of horror and absurdity, he is my *memento mori* in a greasy green-blond wig.

People are a little alarmed by how taken I am with this character. *This* is the film where I find my solace? But as the Joker himself puts it, "Whatever doesn't kill you"—tongue swipe—"makes you stranger."

Possibly I am becoming strange. Sometimes I feel the Joker's merciless mask on my own face. I am tempted to draw the lipstick out past the edges of my mouth and stop washing my hair. Dramatic suffering, tales of horror, obscene and terrible losses—now they feel like home. In their shadows I feel less an anomaly. I am drawn to the dark not ghoulishly but as some kind of deep, even holy, recognition of the presence of the unholy in life, the ubiquity of outrageous suffering.

A story in the local paper catches my eye. It concerns Linda Chase of Jackson, Michigan, and her longtime companion, Charles Zigler: "Chase, 72, and Zigler lived together for 10 years. In December Zigler died in his sleep at age 67. Instead of letting go of her good friend though, Chase ended up keeping him in the chair in which he died." They watched NASCAR together. "I didn't want to be alone," she says. "He was the only guy who was ever nice to me." He could always make her laugh, she says. She kept him clean, she says; he didn't smell. "It's just that after so many bad things happen to you, I don't know."

I don't either.

✷

My mind is still a minefield. I move around it cautiously. I can acknowledge that Bob is dead, and I can feel the weight of grief. I can say to myself the facts of his death and even remember the officers using the word *deceased*. But my mind cannot go near the river. I veer away before I see the slipper under the big pine and know with utter certainty where I'll see the other one. I start to approach the water itself, remembering how it felt, how cold and strong its current, and I pull myself away. These areas have a radioactive glow about them. Nearing them, I feel their pulsation. They are stronger than I am. But there is one forbidden place above all: the place where I imagine Bob falling, terrified, drowning. I pray (to what?) he had that heart attack, somehow lost consciousness before he hit the water, but I don't allow myself to imagine this, or the alternatives. I take myself—consciously, intentionally—by the shoulders and steer myself away from these places. I keep myself within a small space surrounded by an electric fence, like a dog learning her limits.

✷

One bright day I am out in the front yard, pulling weeds, when Con appears. We have worked together for thirty years. His wife's memorial service was the same day as Bob's. He has walked over from his house, several blocks away, though he is not in full health himself and is stricken by Marion's death. He is the kind of man, theirs the kind of long marriage, where the woman's death somehow drains the color from the man. Yet he wears his sorrow gently, the grief of an old man who accepts his lot. I envy him. He says how sorry he is for me; I say the same for him. "Oh," he says, "but Marion lived a good long life and we had a long time together. What's happened to you is terribly unfair." We sit together for a while in that truth, in the sun on my front steps.

Zaide and John show up at my back door with two large planters full of flowers, the only ones I will have this summer. This inaugurates a tradition of almost weekly dinners at their home. When I break down, Zaide silently comes behind me and puts her hands on my shoulders as if she's holding me to the earth. John takes my hand and says the Holy Spirit is with me.

"But I don't believe in the Holy Spirit!" I wail.

Without a beat, he says, "The Holy Spirit doesn't care!"

And through my sobs, I am laughing.

I have never accepted so much from others, never had to. Despair reduces me to some common denominator, sometimes uncomfortably so. As Lear says of Poor Tom, I am "the thing itself: unaccommodated [wo]man . . . a poor bare, forked animal." I feel abject, abashed before people's kindness, as before cosmic cruelty. I ponder the word: *kind-ness*. I remember learning in my college Shakespeare course that in the sixteenth century, it retained some of its original sense: *being of one's kind*, being of the same ilk. To be *kind* was to be *kin*, to behave with another person as if you were related. Sometimes, in the presence of this kindness, I feel the dreadful isolation draw back from me for a moment, and I am almost human.

✳

"The worst," says Diane. "We've been through the worst."

Our friendship is old, riddled with uncanny parallels. The latest is this "worst," two distinct nightmares ravaging the first decade of the new century. Hers is a child who is a severe addict, in whose ongoing life she can never fully believe. Mine is a husband of four months who disappeared into a river. Hers is the zombie nightmare that drags on, refusing to die. Mine is the sharp, stunning explosion, brief and so horrible wakefulness can't shake it.

"No," I whisper, weeping. "Not the worst. Darfur is the worst."

In Darfur, in western Sudan, women in a refugee camp have a daily choice: they can walk to get firewood and water, but if they do, they will be attacked and raped by the government-sponsored marauders known as Janjaweed. The sole third option is to die.

To suffer in a world of suffering. If only you could take your place among the sufferers and find solace there, but you don't, necessarily, or not for a very long time. You also don't back humbly away from the vast suffering you see and say, "My pain is nothing to this." Because your pain isn't nothing to anything. Unfortunately, what you often do is weigh, measure, compare. It's senseless but unavoidable. Perhaps on some level it's the mind's struggle to integrate the enormity it has experienced into some larger scheme. You hear of a calamity and think, "That's worse than mine" or "That's not as bad as mine." You meet a fellow sufferer and wonder how his heart compares to yours. You do this for a long time, possibly forever.

The Widows' Club clusters around me sometimes, trying to initiate me. The women who say, "I lost my Gary last year. Cancer. We were married forty-three years"—I want to slap them. It's all I can do to be civil, commiserate nicely. In my head, I'm raging. *You had him how long? And cancer, so you knew it was coming? And you're seventy-eight? Bitch, please!* A young friend loses her mother and I'm torn between putting my arms around her and folding them across my chest. *Parents, yes: they die. I've lost several. You're supposed to bury your parents. It's how life works, at best.* This hardening of the heart shames me, and worries me too: will the calcification set in for good? What is becoming of me?

I find unhealthy solace in a catastrophe worse than mine. It makes me feel less obtrusive, less freakish. In the sharpest of ironies, Bob gave me Joan Didion's *The Year of Magical Thinking* for our final Christmas, a week before we married. Now I think back on it. *Yes*, I decide, *that was worse—losing a husband and a daughter in one year.* Then I wonder: *Would it be worse to watch your husband collapse at the dinner table or to run screaming through the dark praying he's not in the river and knowing he is?* It amounts to something like the medieval considerations of angels on pinheads, but it's almost compulsive. I am trying to place myself in the ranks of the bereft. I am trying to find my place in the columns of losers and lamenters. I am trying to make my disaster human by working it into the endless tale of human horror. In some strange way, this is part of approaching the land of the living.

✳

In September, as school starts, I reenter my life with some surprise that it's still there. I walk around it, doing what I'm supposed to be doing, trudging through my days or floating through the hours like a ghost. I cry so readily, so frequently, that I must be on guard. I am, in Colm Tóibín's words, "wandering in a sea of people with the anchor lifted, and all of it oddly pointless and confusing."

Grief is not pure; it's not just pain. This grief, my peculiar animal, streaked as it is with trauma and rage, has mass and weight, as I learn from my constant exhaustion. Like much grief, it is curdled with guilt: in one of the forbidden places in my mind dwell all the ways Bob's death was my fault, and all the ways I might have saved him. I creep to the edge of that place and back off.

Finally, grief takes the form of a water table: ordinary life is a ground I walk, beneath which the groundwater level is so high that my footprints immediately fill. I feel myself living on a vulnerable surface above a flood that constantly threatens to rise and drown me.

At work I worry about the short-term memory lapses I'm experiencing and also about how easily I tire. By midafternoon I am exhausted. But I am glad to be back, glad the terrible summer is over, glad to find myself capable of presence with my students. I am grateful that this work still matters. Though the entire campus knows what's happened to me, mostly no one speaks about it.

At the end of the first session of one of my courses, a student I don't know waits to ask me a question. She sits down beside me. She is slim with long blond hair, and the open kindness in her face strikes me. Her voice is gentle. I answer her query, she thanks me, and then she leans in and says quietly, "Also, Dr. Griffin? I wanted to tell you how sorry I am for your loss." Instantly the exhausted phrase is newborn from her throat.

My eyes fill as I thank her. Her name, she has told me, is Sara, but as I put my arms around her, the word that comes to me is *grace*.

✷

I spend Election Day ferrying students to and from the polling place assigned to our campus. The ones without cars tend to be the younger students, the first-years, voting for the first time. Their excitement about casting votes for Obama ripples the air in my car.

That night I watch the returns. I think how pleased Bob would be—he decided for Obama last January when I was still with Hillary. I think how my mother would have been gaga for Obama, for all the right and wrong reasons. At 11:00 NBC calls it; seconds later the phone rings. It's Zaide, calling from Democratic headquarters downtown, and we shout and cry into our phones. I watch the crowds in Chicago, Jesse Jackson's face convulsed in tears, the Obamas walking out under the lights, and I am sobbing. Although I am crying for my beloveds who cannot see this, my tears also have a component of joy, of futurity, of hope.

✷

I am still wrestling with Yahweh when I chance to read about Oya, a Yoruba *orisha*. Weirdly, she is associated with a river—the Niger, the great river of West Africa. She is known as goddess of storms; the tornado is her whirling skirt. But in a larger sense, she presides over change and transition, passages from one state to another. She is celebrated as the spirit of clearing-the-way, just as the tornado whips through a ponderous hot afternoon, sweeping worlds away, ushering in clear, cool air. Beautifully, terribly. Oya's home place is cemeteries, where she clears the way for the living to cross through the doorway of the grave to what lies beyond.

Sometimes, fleetingly, I feel something like that clearing effect. My gutted world feels like a big house that has been radically blown clean. So much is beyond my control that I keep giving up, opening my hands, releasing things, letting go. So little matters that what does matter stands out clearly. So much is fearfully difficult and I am so diminished that I do what is doable and easy and I abandon guilt about my limitations, because that's too much to carry. I care less than ever in my life about being good and living up to something. Dilemmas resolve quickly. Priorities arrange themselves effortlessly. The heart speaks with unusual clarity. Though living is immeasurably harder, life seems simpler.

I am nervous in crowds now, and made anxious by noise, so I pursue solitude and silence. I experience a new level of intolerance for confusion, obfuscation, bureaucracy, bullshit, but a new tolerance for many human foibles. Also, I now have the psychic version of Superman's X-ray vision: I can see straight through bluster and aggression to the fear and vulnerability cowering behind them. Everybody is Poor Tom, a lone suffering bastard, and if they aren't, I haven't got time for them. I am drawn to suffering like birds to my feeder: I crave the company of the grievers. I must be among my own. I need to stand on the ground where compassion arises. Otherwise, I am alone again on that terrible shore.

✳

"The deepening of the heart," says Mark Doty, "the work of soul-making goes on, I think, as the world hammers us, as we forge ourselves in response to its heats and powers. The whirlwind pours over and through us, above and beyond human purpose; death's deep in the structure of things, and we didn't put it there."

Recently someone asked me, fear vying with hope in her eyes, whether some new knowledge of myself had come out of my catastrophe. She was nearly begging me to assure her that there was some kind of redemption. I don't remember what I said. I should have said, "There is the deepening of the heart." And it comes through the ongoing making of us, the heat, the hammer, the forge.

Emily Dickinson uses the same metaphor in the wondrous poem that begins, "Dare you see a Soul *at the White Heat?*" It ends this way:

> Least Village has its Blacksmith
> Whose Anvil's even ring
> Stands symbol for the finer Forge
> That soundless tugs—within—
>
> Refining these impatient Ores
> With Hammer, and with Blaze
> Until the Designated Light
> Repudiate the Forge— (#365)

I have always thought of this as one her many poems about the creative process itself. It now seems to me to subsume that story in a larger one—Doty's story about the way *we* are created and re-created, blasted, melted down, hammered, and forged not into some final shape but continuously, all our lives. If I project my earlier reading against this later one, I can contemplate the relation between the processes of living and of creation in a context of damage, violence, the fierce white heat blanching its subject into malleability.

It starts to seem to me that life comes down to a terrible challenge: to participate in the creation, to accept the new form you are taking, even when it is the product of a nightmarish violation. To suffer the deepening of the heart that comes only from profound wounding, vivid ore.

✹

In the spring, as the first anniversary approaches, I teach Coleridge's *Rime of the Ancient Mariner*. I herd the students away from Christian symbolism toward something much more interesting: the Mariner's curse, compulsive narration. As he wanders the world, he is periodically possessed and overcome by his outrageous experience:

> . . . at an uncertain hour,
> That agony returns:
> And till my ghastly tale is told,
> This heart within me burns.

He must disgorge his story to chosen strangers, after which he is left free—but only until his tale rises again, like magma, demanding utterance. On to the next hapless auditor.

I can't bear to tell the story of that night, and I can't bear not to. To tell it takes me so close to the river's edge that my stomach churns and clenches; not to tell it is to stand in a cocoon of silence, watching the world sail away. I tell it to establish who I am now: the person to whom this occurred, the one who has lived, is always living, through *this*; the person who has this memory in her head, and this great rift across her life. And I tell it to bring it indoors, into the realm of language and experience where it can begin to work its way into my story, my being. As long as it remains in the hallucinatory realm, so do I. Yet telling it will always feel perilous, vertiginous, as if I am about to drop into my own maelstrom.

The hapless Guest—drawn off-course on his way to a wedding as I was yanked off-planet on my way from a wedding—is said to wake the next day "a sadder but a wiser man." But sadness seems an odd response to the outlandish story. And what wisdom could he possibly have taken from it? Certainly not the tidy morsel offered by the Mariner:

> He prayeth best, who loveth best
> All things both great and small;

For the dear God who loveth us,
He made and loveth all.

Anyone who has come through the preceding six-hundred-line psychedelic nightmare must find this homily utterly inadequate, even contradictory. This quatrain is a lid clamped down on a wild and untamable genie. Possibly, as he walks away, his evening plans wrecked, the Wedding Guest thinks, "Bullshit." Perhaps his new wisdom, not to mention his sadness, rests in his understanding of how much of our life lies beyond the perimeters of meaningful storytelling and homely beatitudes.

The plot of the Mariner's story is circular, as is his voyage: his ghost-ship circumnavigates the globe. The story itself is circular, an endless loop, eternally begun again. And finally, the meta-story of the Mariner forms a larger circle: there is no end to his traipsing around the world, watching for the next proper auditor and telling his tale in order to be temporarily released from his curse. No ultimate redemption from circularity waits—none that we know of, at least. There is only the story, rising up and wanting out. The Mariner casts it out like a fishing net, dragging some poor sucker into a kind of bondage. Telling the frightful story is his way of establishing kinship, affirming himself as human and rejoining the tribe—but just for a time. When the story ends, the Guest goes home alone, newly isolated, forgoing the party. And the Mariner, homeless and estranged, keeps on moving, in search of a version of the story that will cause the chaotic to cohere. His life will clarify like still water, and he will be released.

As I stood in the cabin on that sun-struck May morning, a scrap of clear thought wafted across my mind: *Jesus, now I'll have to write about this.* And so I do, but not the full story. I can never reach the full story; I get to the brink of language and see only deep space before me. Mark Doty writes of mourning his beloved, "There are times I feel I'm translating, in my head, from one language to another; I've become a citizen of grief's country, and now I don't easily speak the old tongue I used to know so well." But maybe the problem, as any speaker of two languages knows, is that some things don't translate; there are no words. Like the Mariner, I try to tell what happened, but when I try for the meaning, what comes out is something lame, like "He prayeth best, who loveth best." So I move on, telling and telling it, hoping to hear the words I need.

. . . and when they go, everything
goes—the earth, the firmament—
and love stays, where nothing is, and seeks.

—Sharon Olds, "Everything"

"WRITE A POEM IN THE VOICE OF A WIDOW WHOSE HUSBAND HAS DROWNED"

(a prompt by Maura Stanton)

What does a widow's voice sound like?
A low wind?
A lowing manatee?
A lowly inmate laughing like a loon?
The hinges of a door everyone keeps forgetting to oil?
A bird of prey?
Something drowning?

"Invent any story you like."

If you wind up with one you don't like, write another.
Use your imagination, that's what we're here for.
Did her husband perish in pursuit of a great fish?
Does the fish really have to be white?
Was he trying to swim the English Channel?
Trying to save a child who had not waited a full hour after lunch?
Is he a hero? A fool? A victim?
Maybe it turns out he didn't drown at all:

Did he fake it and run off with a green-eyed bartender?
This widow, was she a real ballbuster?
Did she marry him for money? Power? Fame? Security?
Do you imagine these are different?
How long was she married to this drowned man?
Would you believe four months? No?
What would you believe? What serves your story?
Use your imagination, but make the story plausible.
No one will buy him fiddling with a bird feeder hung out over a
   high bank.
The isolated cabin? Been done and done.
Do not have the widow discover one slipper below the feeder.
Or if you must, please don't put the other one below, by the water.
Knowing how much is too much, such an important part of the
   writer's craft.

"This is an exercise in empathy."

Can you get inside the head of this woman?
She might be from another planet, where husbands are specters
   and water is deadly and the years gape like mouths and some-
   thing is always screaming.
Do you care about the widow?
Do you blame her for not searching for him harder? Sooner?
Do you care about the husband?
Do you blame him for his preoccupation with bird feeders?
Do you care about the fish, the kid, the bartender, the English
   Channel?
Do you care about the water?
How deeply do you care? How deep is the water?

"How does the widow feel about this particular river or lake or ocean?"

First, let's get specific: is it river, lake, or ocean?
What is its name, in what indigenous language?

Does she refuse to look at it?
Does she want to drain it dry?
Does she see it as her enemy?
Does she see it as an angry god?
Does it tempt her?
Does she want to marry it, marry it, marry it?
How do you feel about water?
Does it ever scare you?
Does it ever tempt you?
How well can you swim?
Can you imagine drowning?
Can you imagine a husband?
Can you imagine a widow?
Can you imagine?
Can you?

HEARTBREAK HOTEL

Once I went with Bob to San Antonio, where he had a conference. While he conferred, I wandered, scrutinizing the Alamo and hunting down Mexican ceramics and folk art. I've always been especially drawn to the *calacas*—the skeletal figures in two and three dimensions, dressed spiffily and placed in all manner of tableaux: a red-frocked singer fronts a band, a happy couple dances. Weddings and marriage constitute a common trope. The shifty irony embedded in the art form fascinates me. I can never figure out if death is being mocked by ordinary human life, or if death is having its day, mocking human pretensions and institutions.

I bought a Christmas scene enclosed in a box, glass on its front and top. Six figures celebrate a *fiesta de Navidad*, four dressed elegantly, two inexplicably naked in their bones. All of them extend one hand, as if grasping an invisible glass. A clock hangs on one side wall, a radio on the other. Lining the back wall are portraits of saints, the Holy Virgin, and the birthday boy himself, along with a large decorated wreath. A skeletal dog lies under a table spread with plates and bowls of food. Along the back wall are candles—and a skull, so that the dead can contemplate themselves, I guess.

As I move into the fall after that first dreadful summer without Bob, Christmas begins to look a lot like this.

✳

Of our eighteen years together, Bob and I spent sixteen in different time zones, so summers and Christmas counted heavily—the two seasons when academics can break loose. But Christmas was initially a site of struggle. He would have been happy to have nothing to do with the American version of The Holidays for the rest of his life. I convinced him that Christmas is like Christianity: not inherently loathsome, only rendered so in practice. So we agreed to reclaim it. Gently but firmly we pushed families away and took our own direction. When Bob was in his second Gold Hill cabin we found a tree stand among the junk piled up in a storeroom, bought a tree, and decorated it with pine cones edged in gold spray paint. With white lights it was perfect shabby Martha Stewart.

I can't imagine a way to endure this year's holidays. The homes of family and friends are readily available to me, and also impossible. I would be doubly trapped, by my grief and by someone else's routines, possessions, floor plan, kindness, traditions, and holiday cheer. I cannot bear any of it. So in late October I put Bob's travel agent to work. The Caribbean, I say; maybe Jamaica.

Why? The Caribbean is not my place. My notion of a beautiful beach is Lake Michigan, and wonderful weather is between sixty and eighty degrees. I hate the whole concept of a resort, and I have never owned anything like the requisite wardrobe—or body. I dislike sitting in the sun. Rum and tequila sicken me; in warm weather I drink gin and tonics, strong, sharp, and icy. But I went to Negril twenty years ago and what I crave now is what I experienced then (minus the unfortunate reaction to a brownie containing preternaturally potent local ganja). I want exactly that feeling of being not where I belong but in Neverland. I remind myself that Neverland is one of the imperialist fantasies that have preyed insidiously on those islands, but I don't care. I want to bury myself in something wholly unlike my reality until the freaking holidays go away.

It is late to be booking for Christmas, but the agent knows the situation and finagles me ten exorbitant days at the fabled Jamaica Inn in Ocho Rios. I try to make a fiction of the trip, to think of myself as some kind of romantic refugee from darkness and horror into dissipation and mindlessness. My imagination has always saved me; maybe it will fly me right over the worst and land me in a new story.

✳

The night before I am to leave brings what midwestern meteorologists call "wintry mix"—precipitation combining with temperatures hovering around freezing to yield rainy snow, snowy slush, slushy ice. My flight is delayed and I miss my connection, which is in Memphis, of all places. There will be no getting out of the country tonight. Memphis is gray and damp. The Holiday Inn near the airport turns out to be a strangely cavernous, grim place with what seem unusually long hallways reaching in many directions. There seem to be few guests, who all apparently know each other; the lobby echoes with talk and laughter. My room is at the far end of one of the long, empty corridors. I drop onto the bed and feel myself float away from my body and dissipate. I've escaped my life all right, and now I'm in a Stephen King novel.

It's just a motel room, I tell myself, yanking my spirit back. The thing to do is get out of here. I consider the options on a dark near-Christmas day in Memphis. The blues seems appropriate. But a woman traveling alone, utterly ignorant of the city, probably shouldn't head down to Beale Street for the evening. So what else is in Memphis?

Surprisingly, it takes me a few moments. Then I grab my second wind, hike to the lobby, go outside, hail a cab, and say, "Graceland."

The car radio reports that an Iraqi journalist threw a shoe at President Bush at a Baghdad press conference two days ago. The driver and I emit simultaneous chuckles. On this trip I am reading Anne Lamott's *Plan B*: "I feel that we began witnessing the end of the world in Slo Mo once George W. Bush became president." The end of the world, oblivion: what a comfort.

✳

It's true: the first thing that strikes you about Graceland is how small it is. You are expecting Tara, and it's more like the biggest house in a ritzy 1950s suburb called Tara Hills.

The weather and perhaps the holiday season have kept the tourists away except for me and a group of Japanese visitors. They are working with a translator, leaving me essentially alone to wander and ponder. The house is glaring in its sheer ugliness, beginning with the white living room with royal blue and gold drapes and huge peacocks etched into the glass panels flanking the opening to the music room. I feel my northern middle-classness sharply: to Elvis, this was elegance. Gladys's bedroom, white with heavy royal purple portieres and bedspread, was his way of crowning his mother queen of his universe.

My audio tour headset features the princess of this weird kingdom, Lisa Marie herself, who shares reminiscences about particular rooms. In the living room she says she knew her father was coming downstairs by the jangling of his bling. In the kitchen, dark with ugly patterned carpeting, she fondly recalls him and his minions cooking up a storm in the middle of the night. What was she doing awake? I wonder. She tells her stories as if they were episodes of *Ozzie and Harriet*, as if her years in a vacuum-sealed funhouse operating in its own time zone constituted your normal American childhood.

After the luxurious whiteness of the front rooms and Gladys's bedroom, the rest of Graceland reminds me of Disneyland— every room a different world. A half flight of stairs down from the kitchen is the Jungle Room, a porch that Elvis enclosed and turned into an ugly little explosion of exoticism, all carved wood and faux animal hide. Whether we're in Africa or Asia or South America is irrelevant: we're Elsewhere, and it's carpeted in a sickly green. Lisa tells me that it later became a recording studio—hence the carpet on the ceiling. Downstairs, on the basement level, are two rooms that constitute a man cave of sorts—Elvis's playrooms. A black and yellow migraine of a room harbors the bank of three TVs that Elvis used to shoot out on occasion. The room across the hall is mostly taken up by a pool table. What strikes me about both rooms is that, although they are already in a basement, Elvis has taken pains to make them seem even more enclosed and bunker-like. The TV room has mirrored walls, which supposedly enlarge a small room but to my eyes simply make it more claustrophobic: I'm trapped there with myself in an endless reiteration of that very room. The poolroom's walls are covered in pleated print fabric, floor to ceiling, like one big curtain keeping something hidden. Possibly the décor is meant to suggest a private men's club, or maybe it just hides the furnace. If the front rooms announce the King, these lower spaces, disconnected from each other visually and emphatically self-enclosed, point to someone else, someone who wanted more than anything to hide. I can't breathe down here, but I get it.

I head outside, where the rain has let up. There are a passel of Elvis outbuildings to wander—Daddy Vernon's office; buildings full of cars; the racquetball court now lined with gold records and awards; and the reliquary of memorabilia that I will recall mostly as the Hall of White Jumpsuits, though it also contains the baggy gold blazer I always considered his coolest item. I head for the Meditation Garden. Given the fountains, the towering granite Christ, the proliferating bright plastic flowers, the religious figurines, and the large pictures framed in sharp red and blue, it is hard to imagine anybody meditating here for an instant. There is a quartet of graves—Vernon, Gladys, Elvis Aaron, and next to him his twin, Jesse Garon, stillborn a half hour before his brother. Does it mark you even in pre-consciousness, to be linked to a dead body as you float in the amniotic sea? What did it mean to Elvis to be a surviving twin, those who are said to pass through life with the constant sense of someone missing?

Jesmyn Ward writes of "grief constant as a twin."

I'm trying not to think about how much Bob would enjoy this, how we'd process it all, how it would become part of our common frame of reference.

Instead, I am trying to imagine my way into the strange life of this place. The official narrative here is insistently triumphant, but I always see the Elvis story as a classic American tragedy. It feels utterly weird to be here, where no one I know could possibly imagine I am. But something surreal in the place also feels right. Not Disneyland or Dreamland, and utterly *sans* Grace: more like Nowhereland. Making all my nowhere plans for nobody.

Are you lonesome tonight?

✳

Early the next afternoon my plane lowers into sunny, vibrant Montego Bay. A driver from the Jamaica Inn is there to retrieve me. It's a nearly two-hour drive; I am a day late, and having driven over yesterday to fetch me, he is not happy about this, as if I could have managed better. On the road to Ocho Rios along the north coast, there are white egrets near the water, goats everywhere. A town called Lilliput. A shop called Da Endz. The shops—huts of corrugated tin, mostly, with Coke signs—remind me of West Africa. The driver notes points of interest: "*Discovery* Bay," he says, pronouncing the italics. "Where Columbus landed." And then its perfect complement, Runaway Bay, an escape route used later by enslaved Africans, the maroons who headed for the hills whence they organized their resistance.

For about fifteen minutes after arrival, my spirit lightens. The Jamaica Inn is stunning—long, low blue and white buildings with open-air patios and arresting tilework facing a perfect little half-moon bay. Built in 1950, the inn is for grown-ups. It is haunted by legendary guests: Noël Coward, Katharine Hepburn, Errol Flynn, Ian Fleming. Perhaps in honor of the latter, portions of *Dr. No* were filmed here. Marilyn Monroe and Arthur Miller honeymooned here. At one end of the wide white beach is the restaurant and bar, at the other, on a hill, the spa. My Veranda Suite consists of three spaces: a sleeping room entirely swallowed up by a huge, heavenly bed on which each morning the maid leaves a white towel twisted into the shape of a swan; a bathroom; and a patio/living room, walled on three sides, open to the beach on the fourth. Breakfast is dropped off here every morning. Beyond, a wide white strand, and then the curling, unnaturally turquoise surf.

"All wise people say the same thing," Anne Lamott promises me: "that you are deserving of love, and that it's all here now, everything you need." Possibly this is what I was thinking when I booked—that I would treat myself as if I were a person deserving of comfort. Now I look around at this exquisite world, unreal and alien as Graceland. What is it I need? Why am I here? What exactly am I planning to do with ten days?

I am going to write, of course, but I don't, because I can't manufacture sequence or sense or even interest. Being waited upon by silent, impassive black people makes me just as uncomfortable as it should. Even the other guests make me anxious when I walk the beach. I imagine how I look, what they think I'm doing here, how pitiful and humiliating my aloneness is. On the night of the beach barbecue party for all guests, I hunker down, eyeing the blazing bonfire, fearing that someone might come to fetch me. I feel highly visible and completely invisible. One day I submit to the spa and get an expensive facial that leaves me greasy. I don't even visit the bar. Occasionally I go up to the restaurant for a meal; more often I order room service, along with fifths of Tanqueray at monstrous prices. A friend has given me an ancient iPod, which I've loaded with pulsing classic rock to chase out the wailing in my head. Reading has continued to prove the single reliable antidote to waves of despair and sickening flashbacks to the night of Bob's death, so I finish Lamott and plow through the other books I've brought. Usually water calms me, but when I watch the big, roiling breakers, I keep thinking of Edna Pontellier on the winter beach at Grande Isle. I wonder how far I'd have to swim before I was too tired either to keep going or to turn back.

A dynamic town pulses a few blocks outside the gate, but where am I going to go? With whom? And how? The prospect of venturing out alone in a taxi is so confusing that I quickly abandon it. I realize I feel trapped, paralyzed in paradise.

Another Christmas floats behind my eyes, in another tropical latitude. Bob was working in Massachusetts then. He rented a place in Marathon, halfway down the Florida Keys. I spent Christmas with my parents, planning to fly down to join him the next day. Out of nowhere some savage intestinal ailment attacked, and I spent Christmas Day in the bathroom while it tore through my system. Refusing to consider postponing my flight, I loaded up on drugs and told myself it had been a twenty-four-hour demon.

Bob picked me up in Miami, where he'd spent the night in his car in a parking lot (after having secured the permission of the local police, as only Bob would do). After the long, slow drive down U.S. 1, we arrived in Marathon around dinnertime. I'd eaten nothing since noon on Christmas, so I was hungry.

"What about your stomach?" Bob asked.

"I'm fine! It's over, really!" He looked doubtful, but damned if I was going to spend my first night on vacation in a motel room drinking microwaved chicken noodle soup.

At the seafood restaurant, I quickly decided that what was required was a banana daiquiri. Again, Bob looked skeptical. I was nearly done with the tomato bisque when I understood that Faulkner was right about the past. I went running for the restroom and made it just inside the door before my stomach took itself back to zero. Back at our table, Bob was already laughing, generating jokes that would last beyond the length of the trip about my knocking over waiters and giving it all up to a potted palm.

We spent a day strolling the street circus of Key West. We met friends there and toasted the sunset on the wharf. We visited Hemingway's place and met the six-toed cats. We rented a motorboat and took off across the silvery water. We talked to fishermen and ate conch fritters at a waterside bar. We made love in the afternoon on the big bed in the air-conditioning. Bob bought fresh-caught grouper and cooked it in the tiny oven in our closet-sized "kitchen." We watched stars and waterbirds and other tourists.

Travel: I should have known not to try that. I am a woman alone in the world again, unable to move with the security a man provides. Without the particular joy and comfort Bob generated. I will never move with that ease again. In seven months I have aged ten years; I feel shrunken and vulnerable.

And so I pass my ten days in Jamaica doing exactly what I did all summer at home: reading, staring out at the world, and drinking. I am in a place so beautiful that I feel like an oily blot on the landscape, a human sinkhole. A place so insanely romantic that it seems a cruel joke I have played on myself. I am lost. I need my little brick house urgently, viscerally. I want my cat, the television. Within the first two days I am counting down until I can go home. To Michigan, God love its dark, icy heart.

✳

Of course the January weather ensures that my flight into Grand Rapids is rerouted to Detroit, where I arrive too late for anything but resigning myself to a night in the airport. I'm told I may not retrieve my luggage, for what reason I can't fathom and am too wiped out to try. It will go on to Grand Rapids without me. I wait around the airport all night, and just as the blue air is lightening to gray I phone Bob's brother, who lives half an hour away. Brian is a very early riser and a true child of the Motor City in his eternal readiness to hop in the car and drive for hours. He scoops me up and ferries me across the state. In his car, with his solicitous, comical company, I breathe easier than I have in ten days.

And of course my suitcase has not reached the airport in Grand Rapids. I will have to return for it the next day. Right now, climbing into my frozen Honda, I don't even care. The thin sun has broken through, the mercury is up, the roads are dry, and I am on my way home. I stagger into my house an hour later with a shudder of deep relief, like one who has narrowly escaped harm.

The world out there has changed. Its roads are peppered with explosives. Best to stay in, lock your doors, I tell myself. Since May my house has been my outer layer, and I pull it in around me again.

For a long time I don't travel, and in the middle of even pleasant social engagements I find myself anticipating being home and what I will do when I get there.

It occurs to me that I have veered from escapism to agoraphobia, centripetal to centrifugal energy, in a very short space. But they amount to the same thing—running from danger versus cowering from it. I worry about myself: am I turning into a timorous old lady who lives behind her curtains with her cat? Will I never travel again? Is this quietude, this retreat, the beginning of decrepitude, step one of the death march? Is my life over too?

And I can't do anything about any of this. This grief is a beast I must ride where it takes me, and I must learn to live where it drops me. The fantasy of self-creation—so youthful, so American—has met its death blow. Profound grief is a formidable force; like a storm it reshapes the landscape. I will have to live it out and see what I have to work with.

In my misbegotten Christmas flight, I wound up in two successive havens, two dreamworlds, one lurid, one lovely, places where carefully crafted illusion offers itself to tourists for a price. Both were constructed as escapes or, depending on your angle of vision, retreats—from lives of enormous privilege and wealth within which nightmares lurked. I have fled back to the solidity of my home with its earth tones and replacement windows and insulation, cardinals in the snowy trees outside, and a zillion channels to choose from. It keeps me warm and dry and quiet and safe. I know it's another illusion. Maybe a time will come when I can think about that.

THE LINE THAT
CARRIES ON ALONE

SINGLE __
MARRIED __
DIVORCED __
WIDOWED __

Again the multiple-choice test. This time I'm at my ophthalmologist's office. What is the difference between divorced and single, in ophthalmological terms? How does the distinction between single and widowed matter to my dentist? They both want to know, and I might as well tell them—again. I'm not married; in fact I had barely accustomed myself to the fact of being married when I suddenly wasn't, and I am not given to the notion of marriage enduring beyond death. According to these categories I can't claim to be single, although of course that's what I am. I'm not divorced and therefore starting over. I'm the other thing, the final option, the sad story. When I check the box, I always see a figure in the corner of my eye, shrouded and silent. She is alien, the black fairy crashing the party. I don't recognize her.

✳

The morning following the night they dredged Bob's body from the river, I scanned the universe, looking for something sufficient to hold together the shards of me for a while. But that force was unavailable—my mother, not four years gone.

In those hours of moving very slowly, pulling myself from one moment to the next, hand over hand as if time were a rope, I felt her absence as a roaring vacancy where the magnetic core had been. It came as another outrage, for on top of shock-lightning shooting through me and the maelstrom of grief, there was anger, waves of it that kept breaking over my mind: my mother was not on the earth.

She could and would have held it all with me, I was sure, as she had held me gently before her on my stomach in the water, floating backwards while I learned to swim. If ever I had needed her fund of compassion, the sense of endurance and hope she could convey, her practical genius for sweeping into a scene of chaos and setting it to rights, it was on that May morning as I stood alone in the violent light. But before too long, I would have hit a vein of cold steel. I knew this even in my longing for her. It would be a matter of days, maybe weeks, but not months before she would remind me of what she had survived, and it would come at once as command, dare, and threat. In short, the message would be: *Do not be one of those women who crumble.*

Or maybe I was wrong. Maybe this time she would have bowed to superior devastation. This thought actually veered across my mind: *I've finally beaten her.*

✳

She was warned by her father that she would be a young widow. Her suitor was fifteen years older and maybe he appealed as a fatherly figure to a twenty-four-year-old who adored her own father. He was certainly paternal, my dad—paternalistic, patriarchal, pick your adjective. When I asked her why she married him, she said it was because he treated his mother so beautifully. An old litmus test, I guess, from the days when women didn't get to know suitors very intimately: if you want to know whether a man will be a good husband, watch how he treats his mother. My father was a walking American Dream: blond, blue-eyed, square-jawed, Germanic, he left college when his father died and went to work in the steel mills of Chicago. A white boy with an unrelenting work ethic and a mother to support, he pleased the powers that be and his collar turned white for good. A self-made man, as they used to say. When they married he was thirty-nine, a well-heeled businessman selling steel in Detroit—not a bad line to be in as the city became the Arsenal of Democracy for the coming war. If his bride saw the rigidity and conventionality in him, she chose to overlook them or spun them into gold: *He's solid, reliable, principled.*

When I asked her if she ever thought of leaving him, she reacted as if I'd suggested she go to the moon. "No one got divorced then!" Meaning no one of our class. "And I had no money; what would I have done? I would *never* have gone home to my father." Never mind her mother: she would have felt ashamed to burden her father, financially and otherwise, with a daughter who had failed at the career women were permitted to succeed at: making a marriage.

By the time I was in second grade my father was dying of colorectal cancer. My memories of home are filled with his absences— stays at Mayo, trips to hospitals in Detroit—and with resentment of his presence, always severe, critical, chilling. To me he was generally gentle and loving, but it got him no points because I witnessed his effect on my mother and my brother. He died three days before Christmas in 1959, at fifty-eight. My mother was forty-four: a young widow.

His death came as a sad relief after years of caretaking. But now she found herself in a financial and legal wilderness. Her husband had kept her in complete ignorance about finances, one of those ancient patriarchal traditions in which "protection" is the veil thrown over a tangled mass of anxiety, pride, and the need for control. He had taken care of his mother; now he was taking care of his wife. Unexceptionable manly behavior. So she spent a year or so untangling accounts, interpreting numbers, consulting lawyers and bankers, figuring out whether she could keep the house, whether my brother could stay in college, whether I could go to camp. The nadir came when she had to petition the court for legal guardianship of her children. In those dark days this was not merely a matter of filing papers; she was required to demonstrate, before a judge, her moral fitness to care for us: "my *own children!*" as she always put it, outraged all over again, retelling this story regularly as both cautionary tale and exorcism. For my mother, *widow* meant warrior.

✳

An odd word, *widow*. It seems to echo like a vault, its *w*'s closing around it like shutters or heavy wings. It is both noun and verb, but the transitive verb form—*to widow*—is all but extinct. The only form we use is the reflexive: *to be widowed.* To have something radical done to you, by a power not your own. To be changed, made different, by a death. To become not single again, or unmarried, but something else altogether. To be propelled into difference and cast into an outer darkness.

Widow has no synonym. It is also one of very few words in English whose masculine form, *widower*, derives from the feminine. That's how deeply widowhood has belonged to womanhood and how powerfully it has affected a woman's status. But what it lacks in synonyms *widow* makes up for in metaphors:

Widow's weeds: the reverse bridal gown, the manless woman darkly revirginized.

Widow's peak, said to derive from the cap or hood worn by mourning women, which dipped to a point over the forehead.

Widow's mite, linking manlessness and impoverishment.

The *widow hand* in a card game: the superfluous hand dealt and set aside as an option for a player with a bad hand.

Grass widow: an archaic term for an unwed mother (no husband but the grass she lay down on).

Merry widow: the long-line bra-corset introduced by Maidenform in 1955 and named for the 1905 operetta by Franz Lehar. The woman delighted to be disencumbered of a husband, probably having inherited his money

Five-fingered widow: a British soldier's sobriquet for his masturbatory hand.

And of course, the spider with the telling red figure on her back who monstrously widows herself.

At the top of the house is the *widow's walk*, where she paces off her scanty space, scanning a vacant horizon, waiting for her life to return.

Widow evolved from Sanskrit and Latin roots meaning *empty, void*. A woman unmanned: a nothingness.

✳

My mother was what was known as an *eligible widow*—attractive financially and physically. As the 1960s blew away the dust of the '50s, she met a man who presented the antidote to my father. Warm, funny, fun-loving, childlike in many ways, slightly irresponsible, he brought the party into every room he entered. Above all, he adored my mother. She was suddenly having an extremely good time—traveling, drinking stingers, going to the racetrack and out to dinner, dressed beautifully and colorfully. I remember her laughing more than I'd ever known.

Thirteen months after their wedding, one night early in January, his heart stopped. It turns out that his doctor had told my mother he had perhaps five years. She jumped in anyway, betting everything against the odds. But in the long winter months after his death I could smell the outrage roiling through her grief.

With this second widowhood she ascended into myth. She had suffered through my father with a relentlessly stiff upper lip in true devoted-wife style, and then the man who redeemed her heart had lasted just over a year—it was grossly unfair. From that moment until the end of her life, people regarded her with at least a soupçon of awe. The first adjective people used to describe her was *strong*. My word is *formidable*, French or English. She and her noble suffering significantly defined the story of our lives. Other people had mothers; I had an epic warrior queen.

It will perhaps seem paradoxical that she told me more than once that she was "a man's woman," despite my horrified protestations. "No," she said, "no, I'm happiest with a man." In any case, she wasn't alone long. Within sixteen months she was married again, to the brother-in-law of #2, and this one stuck for nearly forty years, until her death. They made a rich, satisfying life together, and she did not have to bury him.

Yet even the satisfied calm of her third marriage did not quell the old outrage. What ignited her furious judgment seemed to be the struggles of a younger generation of women. Daughter, step-daughters, daughters-in-law took the brunt. We had not suffered as she had; we were not bucking up and holding it together; we did not comprehend what life demands of women. If we brought her our dilemmas or sorrows, we never knew which of her faces would meet us: the earth mother or the imperious wicked queen of Disney's *Snow White*. Sometimes they merged just at the point where her endless competence and good sense measured our fallibility.

Just once I got her to admit how much easier she was on men and boys. "Well," she said thoughtfully, "I guess I always thought they needed it more." This was a major epiphany for me: women's lenience toward men, their willingness to make excuses for men and do their work for them—which had riled me since early childhood—came not from respect but from a sense of men's weakness, their incompetence, their dependence (which, of course, it also serves to reinforce). Hers was a generation of women who saw men as requiring looking after, even though (or perhaps because) they were running the world. It was easy to extrapolate: she was hard on women because she thought we could take it— because we *must* be able to take it. She had had to woman up to get through twenty years of terrible marriage, two widowhoods, and a heartbreak; we were expected to do the same.

So when my first important adult relationship was shattered by infidelity, she was compassionate for about ninety seconds, and then time was up. *"Don't you think I've been hurt in my life?!"* The question shot out from nowhere; neither of us had mentioned her or her life. Somewhere inside my anguish I was furious: how could she switch the subject from my life to hers and then make me out to be the unfeeling one—me, the sufferer in the present case? The mother I needed was gone, replaced by the Witch of the West.

I look back on that moment and wonder what my pain triggered in her. It wouldn't surprise me in the slightest to know that she had endured my father's infidelity. But the size of her response suggested more, as her responses to me tended to do. I think that of all female suffering, mine roused her to greatest combativeness because it drew on her deepest love and fear. I was not to be a woman who allowed my life—and certainly not the men in it—to damage me. For me to become anything approaching a victim was not an option, ever. She would burn it out of me with maternal fire.

So it was that on that May morning by the river, finding myself with no warning in the wasteland of sudden, outrageous widowhood, I wanted my mother, but wanted her with an edge of trepidation, of ambivalence. Something monstrous had befallen her girl. But what face would she have turned to me? Her compassionate stalwartness was the only thing that would have comforted me. Nothing else could have taken my destruction in its arms but her ability to convey that she was bigger than any catastrophe. But when I imagined her instead demanding that I consider her own suffering and toughen up, I began to implode.

✳

I remember, when I was first learning computer language, seeing the phrase "widow and orphan protection" and laughing. Shades of Dickens, and Lincoln's Second Inaugural Address. But in fact, *widow* came into usage as a typographical term earlier in the twentieth century, when it was adopted to refer to a line of text that ends a paragraph but appears at the top of a new page. It is considered unsightly, messy, *residual*.

Of course it lends itself to personification. A 1936 article called the typographical widow "that awful slattern of the printed page." *Slattern*: a sloppy girl, etymological aunt to *slut*. Nowadays the typographical widow is described with less censure than pity: "a word or short phrase separated from the rest of a paragraph and left sitting at the top of the next column or the next page"; "widows and orphans are words or short lines at the beginning or end of a paragraph, which are left dangling at the top or bottom of a column, separated from the rest of the paragraph."

Sitting or standing, above all she has been *left*. The 2004 edition of *The Elements of Topographical Style* offers a helpful mnemonic for the distinction between widows and orphans: "An orphan has no past; a widow has no future."

✳

A future requires a past.

I wore my wedding ring for four months, eight days. It is a plain gold band with an inscription on the inside: *Will to Mollie*. Mollie was my father's German mother, Amalia (the one he treated so well), and Will was his father. In addition to the ring, I inherited from my grandmother a set of ponderous old photo albums and a picture of a woman, set in a deep, shining wooden frame with a gilt inner margin. The woman is not young, but her very dark hair, pulled tightly back behind her head and caught in a decorative comb, reveals no gray. The expression in her eyes seems tinged with bewilderment, though it might have been a fleeting effect of the camera's flash. On the back of the frame is penciled "Captain Griffin's mother." Captain William Griffin, Will's father, my paternal great-grandfather, was baptized in Montreal in 1833 and became a merchant seaman on the St. Lawrence River and the Great Lakes. For years this was all I knew of the woman in the imposing frame—whose mother she was.

Then one day, in one of Mollie's albums, I found an envelope containing two folded eight-by-five-inch pieces of scratch paper, browned with time, labeled "The Griffin Family." Covering them are penciled names and dates. I had to read the pages over several times before the story began to emerge.

It begins auspiciously, at the top of the first page, with a marriage announcement:

Edward Griffin & Margaret Kelley Married in
Montreal Oct 22nd 1832

Then a list headed "Births":

William Griffin	*Born in Montreal Dec 1st 1833.*
James Griffin	*Born in Montreal July 12th 1835.*
Mary A. Griffin	*Born in Sackets Harbor Sept 23rd 1837.*
John Griffin	*Born in Kingston June 11th 1839.*
Margaret Griffin	*Born in Kingston June 5th 1841.*
Edward Griffin	*Born in Kingston June 5th 1843.*
Celia Griffin	*Born in Pt. Dalhousie June 5th 1845.*

Next to young William's name, Mollie has inscribed, in ink, "Capt." The woman in the beautiful frame is Margaret Kelley Griffin, and these are her children: seven in thirteen years, a child every two years, according with nature's merciless plan, the last three exactly two years apart to the day. At the bottom of the page the parents' birthplaces and dates are supplied: Edward was born in 1808 in Montreal, Margaret in 1809 in St. John's, Newfoundland. So at their marriage they were twenty-four and twenty-three. They moved a lot, from one end of Lake Ontario to the other, St. Lawrence to Niagara, and across the border to Sacket's Harbor in New York, all at a time when the new Erie Canal had revolutionized traffic to and from what was known then as the "West." They settled in ports, where ships of all kinds brought news and supplies, books and building materials. Edward, a journeyman carpenter, would have found ready work. No wonder their firstborn grew up to sail the waters that dominated his childhood horizon.

On page 2 the story turns. There are just five lines of writing, a terse denouement:

Edward Griffin 1st	*Died Nov 8th 1845*	*Age 37 years + 3 days*
Mary A. Griffin	*Died Sept 24th 1837*	*Age 1 Day*
John Griffin	*Died Jan 15th 1840*	*Age 1 year + 7 months*
Margaret Griffin	*Died Sept 18th 1845*	*Age 5 years*
Celia Griffin	*Died Nov 30th 1845*	*Age 3 months*

How is this story to be told? The information shifts kaleido-scopically, arranging and rearranging itself. Look at ages and you'll discover that the birth and death dates don't match the ages in the cases of John, Margaret, and Celia—hardly surprising when family information traveled intergenerationally, mostly by word of mouth. But Mollie's account of the children's lifespans wouldn't have been far off. Four of seven children lost before the age of six, a breathtaking percentage even in an era of high child mortality. Or look through a gendered lens: all three girls gone, when daughters were often their mother's closest companions and most valuable help. A husband dead before he reached forty, leaving his young widow with what resources, what recourse? Or, finally, look at the particular constellation of dates: in Port Dalhousie, on the shores of Lake Ontario, in the autumn of 1845, Margaret Griffin, having already buried two children, lost her husband and her two young-est daughters in the space of eleven weeks.

Most probably, illness swept through the Griffin house on dark wings that fall. But who knows? Maybe Edward's heart exploded while he was sawing a timber. Maybe little Margaret toppled off a dock, and baby Celia was born with a fatal defect. In any case Margaret was left to bury her dead. And perhaps to study the face in the mirror, suddenly older, with a permanent expression of won-der at what the river could bring to one's door and what those on shore could be required to endure.

Those childhood morality rates would have led any woman almost to expect to lose children, or at least to chasten her hopes that all seven might live to adulthood. Did the knowledge of the odds make the loss easier? Historians used to argue that it did, offering as evidence the fact that the same given name so often reappears assigned to a subsequent child. But instead of indicating lack of attachment, might this practice not indicate the opposite—an attachment to little Martha that survived to fasten to the new Martha? That is, after all, part of why we name children after relatives. What data, really, will tell us how our great-grandmothers lived, inside themselves, bearing children relentlessly, and how they incorporated staggering loss into their own narratives of their lives?

So when Edward died, Margaret was thirty-six—a young widow. Six and a half years after that dreadful fall, in April 1852, she married one John Jones. Near the end of the century, city records find her living alone in Montreal, at least into her eighties. So she buried him as well.

✳

Postscript: Margaret's eldest, Captain William, grew up to sail the Great Lakes into a good old age. He crossed the St. Lawrence and married an American woman. They had two sons. The younger, named for his father and called Will, married Amalia, called Mollie, daughter of German immigrants, in 1898. They likewise had two sons, the younger of whom was my father. In 1920, when the sons were twenty and eighteen, Will died at the age of forty-nine. Mollie was forty-three—a year shy of my mother's age when my father died. Another young widow.

✳

I study Margaret across the years between us. Her photo hangs where I see it every morning and am reminded of the cruelest yet most salutary truth: one's particular experience of shattering loss, the trauma that violently destabilizes one's life, is ultimately as ordinary as joy. I have felt in my own eyes the thousand-mile look in hers. What would she have to say to her precipitously widowed great-great-granddaughter? Would she put her arms around me and sing a song she sang to her children? Put a firm hand on my shoulder and tell me there is nothing to be done, so get on with life? Turn on me and hiss, *"Don't you think I was hurt in my life?"*

In the time after Bob, that last voice rises in me now and then. I know how suffering can shrivel and calcify the sufferer and turn her mean. I've had to swallow my mother's words in the face of other people's calamities, struggling to churn bitterness into compassion. I have better understood my mother's rage, her impatience with the novice sufferer. I study her and all the widows in my family tree as if they were constellated stars. I try to discern a shape, a direction, a story that arrives at myself. I know I am not the conclusion. Stories only "come to conclusions" when we stop talking. Like starlight itself, the tale I have read in the lives of these women reaches me from the past but does not reach any conclusion. It becomes mine to imagine. I'm the one who carries it forward.

"A widow," one source has it, "is a word or line of text that is forced to go on alone and start its own column or page." This is the line I join: the ones who carry on, carry over onto the next page, blank and ghostly as it may be, and, with every ounce of imagination left to them, begin to write.

A CREATURE, STIRRING

It is Christmas night—or, more accurately, 2:00 in the morning of December 26. I am on the small porch at the side of my house. My cat is on my lap. The door to the living room is closed. Every window inside the house is wide open because the house is full of smoke—a vile, stinky smoke. The porch is winterized, but I have opened one window about six inches because of the smoke escaping from the house. And what I am saying to myself is *Well, at least the temperature's up in the twenties.*

The cat is unusually docile. He knows that something fairly strange is going on, and he is cold. I murmur to him over and over that we'll be all right. With sudden crystalline clarity I know that I am absolutely alone in the universe, except for this small animal.

Will it reassure you or just make the whole scene weirder if I tell you that the smoke is from burnt cat food?

✳

During the first year after Bob's death, a member of the Widow Society told me that for her, Year 3 had been the turning point, and so it was for me. The book I had been working on when Bob died was finally published, and people wanted to talk about it, giving me a sense of solidity. The feelings of fragility and endangerment lifted and I walked on firmer ground.

During the fall of that third year, I noticed that when I came downstairs in the morning to feed Scout, his dish was empty. Totally clean, crumbless. This was unusual. He was never a huge eater, possibly because he dined sumptuously outdoors, at least during the warmer months. He had always left a little kibble in the dish overnight. I was mystified: he didn't seem to be gaining weight; I concluded that he'd simply decided the Science Diet he'd been lackadaisically consuming for eleven years was tastier than he'd realized.

Then one day I happened to turn on my oven. When you live alone, you usually use the stove or the microwave. Cranking up the oven to 350 to cook one pork chop just seems grandiose. So I hadn't turned the beast on for a while. As it heated up, smoke began to curl from the lip of the door and the opening between the burners. Now, I'm not conscientious about cleaning the oven, which is to say I hadn't done it in years. But the smoke filling the kitchen didn't smell like the smoke of a dirty oven. It was a dank, burning smell. The smoke was rolling out into the dining room when I shut the oven off and threw open the windows.

When the oven cooled down, I opened the door. Around the oven floor were little blackened piles of what looked like dollhouse-sized charcoal briquettes. Or like burnt cat kibble. One pile in each corner, like ritual cairns. When I pulled out the warming drawer beneath the oven, more of them clattered down into the drawer or out onto the kitchen floor.

I looked down at Scout, who was sniffing the putrid air. *Don't ask me*, he said. *I was wondering where it all went. What, you think I crawled into the oven?* I was a little freaked out: something was afoot in my house (my safe harbor, my refuge) that I couldn't explain, something that obviously involved a living—

Ah.

The previous summer, I'd had a swinging pet door installed in the screen on one of my porch windows, an antidote to the cat's incessant demands. At first, it seemed like a wonderful improvement—I was freed from constant doorman duty. But within weeks, a downside made itself apparent. I had to carry outside a number of feathered or furred creatures that were either dead or soon to be so. One summer day Scout brought home a tiny brown field mouse, quite alive, which quickly shot under a small cabinet. I quarantined the mouse on the porch and made several vain attempts to catch it in plastic containers. Eventually I propped open the cat door to give it a means of escape and went on about my day.

And forgot about it.

I think of myself mostly as a responsible person who looks reality in the face. But in fact we contain multitudes, as Uncle Walt used to say. Among my multitudes is a person who occasionally, when faced with a frustrating problem, closes the door on it and walks away. And keeps going. When I didn't see the mouse again, I happily concluded that it had gone out the same way it came in.

I now understood that as autumn closed in, the mouse had found in my oven the perfect winter lodging. Since it was never turned on, it was simply a large, dark, warm, dry, and undisturbed place to store the endless supply of nutriment that magically appeared across the room in the white ceramic dish every day.

I moved the oven. I banged on it. I shone a flashlight behind the adjacent refrigerator. I swept and vacuumed cat food from the oven. And once again closed the door and walked away. Of course, a day or so later, when I opened the oven door to check, there were three new cairns, and the warming drawer was rolling with pellets.

With a bolt of grief, I thought how much Bob would have loved this situation, or rather, loved attacking it. Like most men, he enjoyed an adversary, however tiny. I grew accustomed to the firecracker sound of mousetraps going off in his relentless war against rodents at the cabin. I would wince, feeling the little necks snap. When I protested that they were welcome to their share of the rice and Cheerios, Bob raised the stakes: they would eat through our electrical wiring! I used to watch conspiratorially as the odd mouse snuck across the living room, with Bob six feet away, absorbed in the newspaper. He insulated me from real moral choices: I could align myself with the victim while he shouldered the responsibility for eliminating the threat.

Now it was all on me. I thought of this little critter tearing around the house, tiny and alone and terrified. Was I anthropomorphizing, projecting my own feelings onto a rodent? Of course I was. But I simply couldn't buy the snap trap. Instead, I got a more expensive black vinyl tubular item that used leverage and peanut butter to trap the mouse, who could then be transported outdoors. Of course the peanut butter disappeared and the mouse was nowhere to be seen. Again I swept, again I vacuumed. Again, again, again.

Doing the same thing repeatedly and expecting a different result is said to signify insanity. Why didn't I just call an exterminator? That this option never occurred to me suggests that I was in fact a little crazy. I'd like to blame it on my postmortem state, but I was dealing with much more complicated problems than mice at work every day. So I must confess that among my multitudes is another person who, when the rock keeps rolling down the hill, switches off her brain, puts her shoulder to the boulder, and makes like Sisyphus. From Sartre's perspective, that's the essence of Absurd. But from the rock-pusher's point of view, what she's doing looks like survival.

✳

The encompassing cosmic aloneness I was feeling on the porch that Christmas night had irrupted into my days with some regularity in the last three years. Before Bob's death, I had felt alone often, powerless sometimes, and truly terrified maybe once. But the night he died, the unholy trinity came to me united, unmediated, unmasked, and when you look them in their empty eyes, they enter you and lodge for good.

From the first, I had been especially on guard as The Holidays approached—hence the disastrous Jamaica trip that first Christmas. I just wanted life to go on without me. The thing is, life keeps calling you back. People want to take care of you. They want to make sure you're not alone—as if that weren't exactly what you are. They want to include you among the living. Above all, they want to make sure you're covered during that ghastly six-week ordeal we call The Holidays.

Intellectually, you can deconstruct them all you want. Morally, you can disdain the orgy of excess. You can roll your eyes every time Andy Williams insists that it's the Most Wonderful Time of the Year. But The Holidays is a tenacious and hydra-headed beast. Deep below the tinsel and overkill, formidable forces lurk, powerful tropes: childhood, the communal feast, the return of the light. If you are painfully alone in December, everyone else is a Who down in Whoville, joining hands with the others to sing, while you lurk up on your frozen precipice, pretending to despise them.

Now, add to the mix the fact that New Year's Eve is your anniversary. Which you never got to celebrate, not once. So what you want to do from mid-November on is to sit under a fleece in front of the TV with a bottle of Dewar's and a cat on your lap, watching Johnny Depp movies and calling for takeout until the bloody year has turned and everybody stops shouting. But your beloved's beloved sister insists that you join her crowd for Christmas Day. You understand—distantly, as one hears the doctor's voice through anesthesia—that human connection is necessary. In spite of yourself, you go about the grim business of continuing to live.

So, yes, I said, I'll be there.

I could barely muster the energy to buy a bottle of wine. I sat in the middle of the festivities feeling like wizened Scrooge at the edge of Fezziwig's party: someone formerly part of the joyful human community, now a ghost, a grayness at the margins. I couldn't understand why no one spoke of Bob, and I prayed that no one would, lest I collapse in sobs. I kept floating out of my body, out of the picture.

With a sickening jolt I realized I had turned into Aunt Etta— my father's aunt. She lived solo in Chicago and worked for her entire adult life in a bank, where she could never be promoted because of her sex. She would arrive some days before Christmas, hair in a bun, tweed-suited, wearing black square-heeled lace-ups and always carrying a lace-edged monogrammed handkerchief. Husbandless, childless, clearly beyond the pale. Some avatar of hers haunts many holiday gatherings. I'm sure single men of a

certain age also suffer through the end of the year, but the uncon-
nected woman is, still, a culturally and socially distinct creature
from her male counterpart. A woman of a certain age, alone, rep-
resents something gone seriously wrong somewhere. She is a spirit
of Christmas Past—residual, a leftover—and of Christmas Yet to
Come, what the young dread to turn into.

When Bob and I were a few years into our relationship, I began
for the first time in adulthood to relax into the holidays—precisely
because Aunt Etta's ghost had been laid to rest. One of the mani-
fold ways I valued him was as a buffer against the terrible aloneness
that lurks in the world, gathering in the corners of celebrations.
Bob made me feel fully part of the human family for perhaps the
first time in my life.

In a heartbeat he was gone, and when I looked into the mirror,
there she was, Aunt Etta, clutching a bottle of wine by the neck.

✴

As autumn of Year 3 leaned into winter, I once again took a deep
breath. As far as I could manage it, I would don my gayish apparel
and show up at my sister-in-law's place in the spirit of Christmas
Present. I shopped for everybody. I bought wrapping paper and
ribbon. I bought several bottles of wine. And I offered to contribute to the feast. A casserole, said my sister-in-law. Something
with vegetables.

So on Christmas morning I got to work. Making sure the oven
was kibble-free, I punched it up to 375. Maybe the heat itself will
drive him out, I thought, and the cat will get him. Hope is the
thing with whiskers.

As the oven heated, it breathed smoke, but only moderately.
The stink was muted. The thing just really needs a good cleaning,
I thought, but I can't do that until spring, when I can ventilate
the house. I cranked open one kitchen window, turned on ceiling
and furnace fans, baked my casserole, and bore it triumphantly
to the party. I drank, ate, drank more, laughed, opened presents
with the requisite enthusiasm and watched them get opened by

others. *Don't wallow*, I told myself. *There are lots more miserable ways to spend Christmas. How'd you like to be at the Gospel Mission or the domestic assault shelter? Woman up.* I reminded myself that "alone" is a highly subjective and culturally bound term; I dug until I hit gratitude for the love of the family Bob had brought me into.

So then, whence came the decision—by all legitimate measures insane—that I made around midnight that night? I can only conclude that it took more than I thought to pull off Christmas Present, and the effort had left me slightly deranged. I like that word *deranged*. Think of it as the opposite of *arranged*: I was out of order, jumbled. Despite the smooth and pleasant day I had passed, I was on some level a mess.

When I got home that night, I watched TV for a while. Around midnight I congratulated myself on another Christmas down and headed for bed. And then, with no inkling that I was about to take a strange left turn, I stopped in the kitchen and decided that the oven couldn't wait until spring. It needed to be cleaned now. Tonight. Wouldn't it be wonderful to wake tomorrow morning to a clean, smoke-free, smell-free oven? Wouldn't it signify a new year, a new approach, out with the old, in with the new? It would. This is what I needed: to take control. So I cracked open the kitchen window again, punched the "Clean" button, and locked the oven door. Scout and I went up to bed.

But I couldn't sleep. I kept my eyes firmly closed, trying to let my breathing deepen, but my alertness wouldn't abate, especially because the smell was now wafting upstairs. Finally, after maybe forty-five minutes, I opened my eyes. Even in the bedroom darkness I saw that the air was thick. I turned on the light and found myself in a fog. I went downstairs into thick white smoke and stench. I could not see the other side of the dining room. The smell was ghastly. I turned off the oven and began yanking open windows. The clock read somewhere past 1 a.m. When all the downstairs windows were open I went back to the second floor and opened those. I switched on the furnace fan and ceiling fans as the cold night rushed into the house.

Scout seemed to be fine, following me around as usual, but I had a sudden, clenching fear: this miasma wouldn't hurt me, but what about something much smaller? The cat's vulnerability seemed urgent. I took him in my arms like a condensed version of my own anxiety and carried him out onto the porch, closing the door behind me. The porch windows were shut tight; a baseboard heater warmed the small space. I settled into a glider chair. The air was much clearer, but the smoke was rolling out under the door, rising like water. Nothing for it but to open a window out here too. Scout wandered around a little, confused, but as the porch grew colder he sought the warmth of my lap.

And there we sit, as you first found us. The house exhales its smoky breath, breathes in the winter night. This is when I give thanks for temperatures in the twenties instead of the teens or worse. I quiet down and sink into the moment: *you're safe, be still, just breathe, just wait.* But I feel like a refugee in my own house. *From* my own house. The cat and I are trapped out here where we originally trapped the mouse (or so we thought), who has now driven us out. This is the last habitable corner of my house, and it's getting colder by the second. My house, my haven in a world where a cold wind howls ceaselessly. Now even my house, polluted and toxic, has expelled me.

What about calling someone? Wouldn't a normal person in such a situation call a friend? I think about it. But what would I say? I don't know a language to make anyone understand my situation. And what would she do? Ask me to come to her house for the night? What about Scout? What is it I really need from anyone at this point? Everyone is too far away, worlds away. I scan my neighborhood and the field across from my house. Everything is dark. Everyone has had their Christmas (except for the rabbi's family on the corner) and gone to bed. They lie under comforters and blankets, breathing clean, warm air, with other people nearby.

Scout and I are the only wakeful beings in the world. Or maybe we have left the world entirely.

In the 1960s, when space flights were always news and astronauts often ventured outside the capsule for some kind of maneuver, I used to imagine being cut loose in space. The horror wasn't asphyxiation. It was being alone out there, left behind, floating unmoored in the cold, dark immensity. In the middle of this blue-black Christmas night, I am as far from the human species as I have ever felt in my life, and as close to the heart of despair. My earlier performance as Christmas Present was brittle and brief; this is reality. This is the Alone I have dragged around forever, as long as I can remember. *If Bob were here . . .* He was a fence around my life, fending off that Alone. For the past two and a half years I have managed to keep it at bay with hard work and good friends and weekly therapy; I have drowned out its howling with booze and TV and books and films and teaching; when I have felt it coming I have refused to look it in the eye. But tonight there's no way around it. The smoke rising from an utterly ridiculous situation has driven me right into its arms.

I rock gently, cradling Scout, warming my hands in his winter-thick fur. I hold him as tightly as he'll permit. "We'll be okay," I murmur. "We'll be okay." After an hour or so I can see the living room ceiling through the glass in the door. I unfold the cat and myself and reenter my house. The smoke is mostly gone. I close windows, turn off lights. As the house begins to warm, we climb the stairs again.

The next morning, the smell is a mild and quickly fading ghost.

A month later I am sautéing something when a tiny brown body shoots out from behind the oven—exactly as Scout walks past. Mouse swings right and makes a good run for it into the dining room, but Cat has got this one. By the time I catch up, the neat little corpse is headless.

"Finally you earn your keep," I tell Scout, gingerly enveloping the body in paper towels.

He eyes me. *And yet you begrudge me the spoils.*

As it turns out, there are people who, for a very reasonable fee, will clean cat kibble from ovens. The one I find says he's done this more than once, which makes me feel slightly less ridiculous. He quickly removes the oven floor and calls me to bear witness to what one mouse is capable of—which, I must tell you, is formidable, especially considering how much kibble I have previously swept and vacuumed, plus whatever the mouse actually consumed. Having discovered the perfect den, the mouse did not kick back and snuggle in. He relentlessly shored away sustenance against future famine. He found his safe place, but it wasn't safe enough. It would never be safe enough. There is not enough kibble in the world, and the Cat always lurks.

✻

Four months later, on a June morning, I was on the porch reading, drinking iced coffee, relishing the light filtering through the newly lush trees, looking up now and then to watch the birds flutter around the feeder. I recalled myself quavering in the same chair, willing myself away from existential panic. December momentarily swallowed June and I shuddered. That night had bloomed darkly into one of grief's monstrous moments, a garish clown in a ghastly dream. These moments colonize you, convincing you that they represent some ultimate reality, the dreadful funhouse asylum to which you are now consigned for life. When you wake the next day, or the day after, to a familiar world where things are the right size and don't want to eat your heart, you are overwhelmed by relief and gratitude, even as you still navigate grief's river. I think this is why people who have lived through a traumatic experience often speak of a new appreciation for small things in small moments: it's not that they've been chastened by life into settling for less; it's that against a backdrop of surreal distortion the quotidian reveals its glory

Of course I had been wrong that night, thinking myself alone in the universe. But of course I had also been right. It's not that isolation and belonging are two halves of one truth; it's that they are separate, coequal truths. That's the hell of it. We are no more alone than one of fifteen sparrows crowding the feeder. We are as alone as one field mouse hunkered down in an oven.

Silky air floated in through the windows, all wide open save the one covering the swinging cat door, now permanently shut. Said door's former user was outside, keeping the chipmunk population in check. How unwontedly quiet and tolerant he'd been that night, curled into himself on my lap. Something in him had comprehended that this was where we had to be for a while, that it was best to be still and wait it out.

It was late morning. Soon the heat would close in over the day like a dome and stay put until 8 p.m., when the blazing western sun would finally begin to melt. Western Michigan is the far edge of the eastern time zone—nine hundred miles west of Boston yet operating on the same clock. We were approaching the summer solstice, when light streaks the sky past 10 p.m. On Christmas night, we had just crossed the winter solstice, the longest night. Even then the dark was beginning to draw back.

Each thing disappears; everything goes on.

—Mark Doty, *Heaven's Coast*

TOWARD WATER

In mind I go to that stretch of Coster Road out past the county
     line,
where its shoulders drop off into swamp, the dead
trees stretching their wracked arms up from the water—
the land of hopeless trailers, walls of plastic sheeting,
ducks and chickens running in yards, a plaster Virgin or small
American flag in a circle of painted stones. At every other
     driveway
an *Exit Realty* sign or some threatening scripture—
not much on mercy, mostly hard choices, immutable fate.
Posted, the trees at intervals declare, *No Trespassing*.
Folks have their half acre of the north and not much else.
When I picture that part of the road, I usually move on
past the alpha and omega, the day care and the nursing home,
where we joked we'd wind up, to where the road narrows,
dropping down to the river, over the small bridge called Rainbow
     Jim's,
the tunnel of pines, and then our driveway curling back
past the weeping fig we planted, hunched and thin
like a starveling refugee landed in the wrong country.

But today I remembered driving the other way, toward town,
that day you spotted the turtle, making its way from water to
     water.
How you swerved, passed it, slowed, pulled over. How you got out,

walked back, lifted it, carried it across, put it down on the bank.
As we drove off, I wondered: does it feel like a god's hands
seizing you, speeding you across the asphalt faster than
you've ever moved, setting you lightly down at the very edge
of your obscure turtle desire? Is it terror you know then,
flying over the ground, or does a nothingness come down
like a shell, stilling you until your webbed feet touch gravel once
    more?
And then life starts to move again, toward water.

The turtle slid into the rest of its life, as we did. That day
we were out for a three-store grocery haul, a good lunch, check
    out
the whitecaps on the bay and home by dark, beyond which you
were headed for the river, the mindless river that gulped you
    down.
It seemed to me I stopped then, but I was only moving
in another layer of time, so slow it felt like stillness.
I was creeping across a long, straight road, a roaring
bearing down on me, no hands to lift me, carry me over.

SINGULAR BIRD

A Discovery Log

1959

My mother saw a great blue heron on the way home from the grocery store. Unremarkable on the face of it; *Ardea herodias* is adaptable enough to live wherever it can find shores and wetlands, Atlantic to Pacific, from as far north as Prince William Sound in Alaska to the Galapagos. So it was not a miracle to see one on the outskirts of Franklin, Michigan, in the 1950s. That didn't keep it from seeming singular.

Franklin was one of the northern suburbs of Detroit born of the first wave of white flight from the city in the early 1950s. They were so new that they contained vacancy: empty lots and fields that didn't yet qualify as lots but for children did qualify as Wilderness, full of cattails and poison ivy and unnamable dry stalks that left you covered in burrs. The real wildness in the vicinity lay in us. We took our adventure where we could find it, and we needed all of it that we could find, for the burgeoning culture of the burbs had as its aim the removal of chaos, the chastening of chance, the settling of the frontier. Our lives were regular, quiet, supervised, enormously privileged and highly predictable. In other words, safe. We knew some fundamental truths: the main course at dinner would come from a limited list of known entrées; we would take piano and dancing lessons; we would be Brownies and then Girl Scouts; for sixth grade we would get either Mrs. Koch or Mr. Polkernowski (aka Mr. Poke, so they rhymed); there were four channels to choose from—2, 4, 7, and also 9, from across the river in Canada; fathers drove off to "the office" in the morning and returned just before dinner; and anybody's mother could be relied on to doctor scrapes, answer questions, hear our news, or drive us home, if she wasn't at the grocery store.

The safety of this disciplined world allowed us to run remarkably free. In summer we flew out the door in the morning and were not seen again until dinnertime. We made the rounds of the neighborhood on foot and bike. But only as far as Fourteen Mile Road, Franklin's northern boundary, which we never thought to cross. Maybe we were under orders from above, or maybe it just would have been like leaving the world behind. There be dragons, in the form of unfamiliar dogs and other obscure dangers.

On the other side of one stretch of Fourteen Mile lay wide acres of dark, dense marsh. This is where one day, driving home from Kroger, my mother spotted the heron. She stopped the car and watched until it flew off. She came home transported. "A heron! A great blue heron!" What happened then was that we mocked her, as we often mocked her enthusiasms, probably encouraged by my father, assisted in turn by an entire culture that consistently presented female enthusiasm as ridiculous.

Why does that afternoon stick in the mud of memory? I keep seeing her, seized by a vision in the middle of her housewifely day, in the middle of her highly prescribed life, in the middle of a marriage that had curdled years ago, to a man deeply invested in his personal patriarchy. Smack in the middle of the century, in the middle of the suburbs of Middle America, an epiphany of sorts. She sits and watches as the tall, thin creature bides its time, waiting for a stray frog, then suddenly unfolds its six-foot wingspan and awkwardly, beautifully flaps the earth away.

1967

Maybe an unremarkable childhood landscape, like a hostile one, attunes you to the remarkable, the irruption of the mythic. I know that I felt it when, at the end of my seventeenth summer, my plane was descending into Portland, Oregon, and I saw through the left window the sharp peak of Mt. Hood—fierce, gleaming, alarmingly close. For the remainder of my visit with my brother and his young family, I kept seeking it on the eastern skyline, presiding like some transcendent, mysterious power.

The Pacific Northwest offered a landscape that spoke a new language. The titanic powers of mountains and ocean in close proximity; the giant firs serrating the sky; the Willamette yielding to the broad, serene Columbia—the vistas were rugged and lyrical at once. I usually visited in summer, so I never saw the legendary drizzle of the other eight months, only the dense greens and florid blooms it generated. I smelled some newness in the air, some openness that encouraged a deep breath. I felt some residue of what the white pioneers might have felt a century earlier, reaching the end of the trail: that life could be reimagined here, as far as you could get from the past.

My brother and his wife lived with their two small children in a house in the West Hills that looked out across the city toward the mountain. They seemed perfect: married, happy, with beautiful children and interesting friends and wonderful places to go and a view of that mountain from the upper story. I felt like an anomaly, as usual. I did a passable impression of a happy teenager to cover a fundamental discomfort, loneliness, and alienation. In my brother's house I was a visitor to a world that I couldn't imagine myself inhabiting.

1792

Admiral George Vancouver, at thirty-five, was enjoying his first command as he crossed the Pacific and turned left, sailing up the western coast of North America. The name of his ship, HMS *Discovery*, reflected his mission and the vision of his age. His Majesty King George III might have lost the American colonies and his sanity, but the British Empire itself was a going concern. Vancouver had two directives: to accept from the Spanish commander possession of Nootka Sound, to the west of the great island that would bear his name; and to explore the coasts in search of that chimera at the heart of so many European adventures, the Northwest Passage.

After confusing and unproductive dealings with his Spanish counterpart, Vancouver sailed south again, into the long, deep sound he would christen after one of his officers, Lieutenant Peter Puget. In fact, Vancouver played to the hilt the Adamic part of the imperialist, slapping the names of his officers or friends on everything he saw. The white peaks rising to the east and south, for instance, were quickly renamed after Lieutenant Joseph Baker, Lord Samuel Hood, the Baron St. Helen's, and Rear Admiral Peter Rainier.

1975

Within five years of my visit, the domestic idyll in Portland had disintegrated, but my brother soon married again. Liddy was a native, born in Oregon, raised in Seattle, graced with a kind of irresistible wide-openness and empathy. Animals and children instantly gravitated to her, and so did I. She had an infallible sense of the absurd, an unerring nose for the comic in any moment. She cried and laughed on a dime, often simultaneously. She voiced her dogs and cats to memorable effect. Her answer to a long day (or, for that matter, a short one) was "Let's have a glass of wine."

Liddy's buoyancy overwhelmed my solipsism and depressiveness. Whereas I tended to obsess over a hurt or a failure as if it were a sore tooth, Liddy's energy was recuperative, forward-moving, light-seeking. She brightened me up and, in a strange way, made me feel saner, as if the world were not entirely fearsome or grim. Her own hurts and losses were mediated by some internal mechanism I seemed to lack. And she liberated me, making me see that rules could be broken, directions ignored.

While my brother practiced law, Liddy and I tore around Portland on random errands, often with her three boys and a large dog in tow and always to the tune of a running desultory narrative of her family, her friends, her childhood. In her tales of growing up in the Northwest, she often mentioned the islands off the coast of Washington—Whidbey and the remoter San Juans, up near the Canadian border. "You love it so much out here; you've *got* to see those islands," she'd say. "Someday we're going. Someday I'm taking you." Over the next thirty years I would visit many times, but I never saw the islands. They floated behind my eyes, out on the water, misty and inscrutable.

1990

Oddly, that describes the place marriage held in my imagination as well: distant, obscure, elusive. Nothing I planned or counted on, another human possibility I regarded as being for others. It was shortly after Liddy's marriage to my brother collapsed that Bob arrived as a colleague at the college where I worked and became a drinking buddy and sparring partner. Yet when his own marriage ended and suddenly we found ourselves "together," it never occurred to me that it might be a temporary arrangement. Bob was naturally more cautious than I and only recently single, after all, so he danced around the edges of my intractable certainty for a while. But eventually, there we were, coupled.

We put in eighteen years, sixteen of them at distances of from seven hundred to twelve hundred miles, as Bob's career took him from New England to Colorado while I stayed safely tenured in Michigan. During that time we rendezvoused once in Oregon (mostly so that he could shield me at a particularly treacherous family wedding), where Bob met Liddy, who threw her arms around him. Neither of us saw a good reason to get married: we were in our fifties, with independent careers and incomes, living time zones apart. Eleven years in, we had had the matching rings designed, agate and white gold, and wore them happily as signifiers of our peculiar togetherness.

And togetherness it was. My earlier relationships with men had been mostly transient. Even several time zones away, Bob was *with* me; I was not alone. I became sharply aware of what being coupled signified to the world, and to me as well, and I paid close attention to the benefits, perceived and real. Hetero coupledom offered safety, social and psychological; I felt I wasn't facing the slings and arrows alone. It offered sexual validation, especially for a woman: despite the gender upheaval of the past half century, the single man is still often seen as enviable, free, a person with options; a single woman registers simply as unwanted. And beyond that, it offered belonging—an official ticket to human adulthood. From pricing to seating to travel to holidays to advertising to dinner parties, the world is arranged for couples. Seeing clearly through the entire institution, I nevertheless embraced it with all my might. Bob brought me a warm new foundation of knowing that I was at the center of another person's life. What I felt, in fact, was *saved*.

1792

In the spring of 1792, *Discovery* anchored on the coast of modern British Columbia. Late in May, Vancouver dispatched Lieutenant Joseph Whidbey, also thirty-five, to explore the sound in a small craft that could probe the inlets, in the hope that one of them would prove to open a water corridor through the continent.

On June 2, sailing the Saratoga Passage along what seemed to be a long peninsula on the western side, Whidbey landed on the southern shore of a deep cove to make some surveys. "Deer playing about in great numbers," he noted, "rich black soil, grass which grew to three feet in height, ferns nearly twice as high, and an abundance of freshwater streams." From all directions people flocked to the water's edge to examine the strangers. He had landed near a large Skagit village; he estimated six hundred residents. This may have been a first encounter with Europeans: Whidbey recorded their fascination with the sailors' skin; he opened his shirt to demonstrate that his pallor was pervasive.

The Skagit replenished Whidbey's stores with gifts of roasted roots, dried fish, venison, and fresh water, and the crew made to depart. But as it turned out, the point declined into a long sandbar. The outgoing tide had left the ship stranded in mud. With the ready help of the locals, the ship was pushed out to where the water took it.

True to form, Vancouver later named the deep cove where his lieutenant had anchored after a friend, a grandson of William Penn of Pennsylvania fame.

2008

Maybe, I thought later, our mistake was tempting some obscure power by trying for too much reality. We had dared to construct a life together, really together, in the same place on the map. We had made it legal, signed documents, bought property, planned a future. But the great cosmic clown revealed itself. Bob's death whipped off the façade of a new life and left me to my old sense of destiny. I was not to be allowed not to be alone. From childhood I had known that isolation was my script, that I was in some essential way *singular*. Now this cataclysm had only reinforced it. A griever is an island.

The world contracted sharply. I reined in my mind lest it wander back to the river and the panic rise again like vomit. I curtailed my life, my movements and contacts. I became insular.

The landscape of time was likewise circumscribed. I couldn't bear to think back to a world with Bob in it; the details of his body, his habits, our times were torturous to recall. Forward was equally dreadful: I had imagined a companionate final chapter; now a wasteland stretched ahead, with nothing waiting. Typically given to regret and worry, now I found myself assertively inhabiting the present moment. Anywhere else was uninhabitable. So for two years, as the initial trauma wore off, I occupied the here and the now as much as possible. I didn't travel. I did my job and came home, dragging grief behind me like a sack of rocks. I tried to turn my new residence in the present to some advantage, and it worked: I found myself more able to respond to the needs of my students and others than I had before. Life felt meager and sad and manageable. And time went past me.

1792

Further north, on June 7, Joseph Whidbey spotted a "very narrow and intricate channel, which . . . abounded with rocks above and beneath the surface of the water." Expecting a dead end, he carefully navigated the tricky waters as they narrowed between rock walls. And then the channel opened and he saw he was wrong: he had reached the top of a long, thin island. He took this information back to the *Discovery*, and in return, Vancouver christened the island after his lieutenant. With the pioneer conqueror's readiness to see the landscape as a willful, untrustworthy opponent, he dubbed the channel Deception Pass.

AUGUST 2010

Approaching Whidbey Island from the north, the road crosses the flat, nondescript terrain around Fidalgo and the Swinomish reservation and then swerves south. Cutting through tall trees, the road suddenly narrows sharply. Without ever having seemed to go uphill, you emerge high above the water. Cars line the roadside and pedestrians wander the sides of the narrow bridge. Far below, indigo waves dazzled by midafternoon sun surge through the brief. rocky passage.

So this is Deception Pass. Less dramatic, less romantic than I'd hoped. It deserves a better story than a British imperialist discovering his misprision. What seemed connected turns out to be separate—really a minor deception at best. Until it happens to you, that is.

Liddy has designed this trip, the fulfillment of the old promise. In the intervening decades she has married again. Her boys, barely out of diapers when I met them, are grown now, two of them fathers. We have both lost our mothers, and I have lost Bob. More recently I lost my left knee, replaced by titanium and still tender six weeks later. Last spring Liddy called to say she was retiring. "So this is it: we're going to the islands! Tell me when you can come; I'll plan everything!" In the days that followed, a remarkable thing happened: I felt myself begin to lean forward.

I left my house at 5:15 this morning, 2:15 a.m. Pacific standard time. Liddy picked me up in Seattle shortly after noon local time, and we've been on the road since then. She has taken the long way, avoiding the ferry to the southern part of the island. So I have been traveling for some fourteen hours. Jet lag is settling in over the basic layer of exhaustion. As we drive down the island I begin to long for sleep. My knee aches from being in one position for hours.

Whidbey is forty-some miles long and skinny, at points just a mile across. To the east you look across to Camano Island, the Saratoga Passage, and the mainland. To the west you see the Olympic Peninsula and the spectral sierra of the Olympic Mountains. The vista constantly shifts: high bluffs looking out over the water, sweeping gold meadows, deep bays, stands of giant evergreens, towns clustered at water's edge. About halfway down, Penn's Cove carves deep into the east side of the island. The cove is famous for mussels; driving around its perimeter you see big wooden mussel rafts floating at the shore. On the cove's southern shore is Coupeville, where we are to meet up with with Liddy's kindergarten friend, Bobbi, who lives here. She tried in vain to find us accommodations until finally, a few days ago, her neighbor agreed to rent us a cottage she owns out at the edge of the cove.

The afternoon turns elastic, stretching on and out of shape. I am struggling to be pleasant to Bobbi and her husband as we run various errands with them, but I feel myself zoning out. When finally we head east out of town at 5:30—8:30 in my body—I've entered some kind of fugue state. I feel like I'm dreaming. The edges of my vision blur; the sun is too bright. I can barely follow the conversation. Restaurants are being considered. God, they want to go out to dinner. I can't imagine doing that.

We turn off onto a side road that immediately dives steeply down into a stand of huge firs, fingering the light. Soon after, another left onto one-lane blacktop with a forbidding PRIVATE ROAD warning in red. The sign reads, "Snakelum Point Road." Suddenly the cove appears below us, wide and bedazzled with sun, and my brain pulls into focus. We're out of the trees and pointing even more sharply down toward the water. At the bottom of the hill the blacktop curves ninety degrees right to follow the shore, rocky and strewn with big drift logs. To the right is a wide, wild meadow footing the high bluff we've just descended; to the left, along the beach, is a line of cottages, nondescript, boxy, close together. We slow to about five miles per hour to pass them. I keep expecting the car to stop or turn, but each driveway is full of cars or kids or dogs. As we pass the last in the row, I see that the road ends at a breakwater and a public beach. I'm confused.

The car stops. Off to the left, by itself out on the very tip of the point, sits a little square house out of another story altogether, a fractured fairy tale. The lower story is covered in dark blue shingles. A squat, dark-gray, four-sided pyramid roof comes down low over the first story like a sorcerer's hat. On all four sides, white-painted dormers look out of the roof like open-lidded eyes. Many windows and doors, trimmed in bright white. Hollyhocks—red, orange, pink—clamber up the walls next to the front door. A dollhouse, a witch's house. I blink and stare. I might be hallucinating.

Inside, it is silent, bright, warm. The peace is palpable. The main room, occupying the left side of the house, centers on a tall, shiny stone fireplace. Next to it is a reproduction of an old photograph of a Native man and woman, reading, "Charlie Snakelum & wife." Through the windows the waters of the cove roll, only a few yards away, below a bulkhead of rocks and standing logs. There is no beach at this point; tide is in and seems almost to engulf the house.

The kitchen, lined with windows, including two original ship's portholes, feels like the prow of a vessel breasting the waves. From the great room, French doors open to a flagstone terrace. In a daze I go out. Across the Saratoga Passage of Puget Sound, Mt. Baker raises its head over a wreath of clouds, reflecting the western light. The White Sentinel, as both the Lummi and Skagit people called it. Sailboats far out. Gulls crying, diving.

I began this day in one world and will end it in another. My sense of unreality, fed by weariness, flows happily into transport.

It is dark when Liddy and I return from dinner. She will sleep upstairs under the eaves; my knee earns me the downstairs bedroom. A queen bed covered in white nearly fills it. Beyond the bed are French doors opening to a patch of flagstones, then perhaps ten feet of grass to the breakfront. The view is straight east, to Camano Island. One of the doors, swollen, won't shut entirely. When I decide I won't worry about that, I feel something open in me as well. I crawl like a refugee onto the bed. I am awake just long enough to take in the lights on Camano, the slight breeze through the open door, the sound of the waves against the breakwater.

1792

It's hard not to watch Whidbey sailing out of Penn's Cove without imagining the locals waving and calling from the shore. A prelapsarian moment: Europe lands in Native America and takes nothing but food, small gifts, help, and data. Native America examines European skin with interest and probably humor, but not fear or worry—yet. Europe sails away, writes in its journal, reports to the boss. Who reports to his. Maps are made, imprinted with the names of Vancouver's associates.

Among the curious, generous people on shore as Whidbey sailed out into the Saratoga Passage, there may well have been a child or youth called Snetlum, who would grow to lead his people. Three years after his death in 1852, two of his sons were among the many signatories of the Treaty of Point Elliott, which began removing the local tribes to reservations to make way for U.S. expansion. The point at the mouth of Penn's Cove remained an important gathering place for the Skagit, imprinted with Snetlum's name, evolved to Snakelum. His grandson, known locally as Charlie Snakelum, is buried there. It was, perhaps, a holy place.

MORNING

Still on eastern time, I wake very early. An orange ball of a sun is rising over Camano into the pale sky. I get up, push the open door wide, and walk barefoot out onto the flagstones.

The tide is far out, exposing the long tip of the point, hundreds of yards of muddy sand covered with shells and weeds. Shorebirds dive and strut, confabulating over stranded mussels and clams. The sun's heat is just a whispered promise through the cool air. The water is silky in places, in others rippled with breezes and complex currents as it breaks around the point. The sun casts a diamond path across the waves. Far out, a ragged wooden elbow rises from the low water, strange relic of a mast, maybe, or a long-gone wharf, now a marker of dangerously shallow water. Farther, a green buoy rocks where Penn's Cove meets the Passage. In the distance, the ridges of the White Sentinel, in shining aloneness above it all, lightly ringed in cloud.

Something on the point punctuates the water: a lone blue heron, on one leg, motionless. Like a dark brushstroke against the morning, more gesture than creature. When it moves, it is with slow, tai-chi grace, one foot down, the other leg bent and drawn up above the water toward its breast, then carefully extended to plant the other foot. Suddenly it strikes like a snake at something in the surf, long neck extending sharply, then whipping back up, tossing the victim down its long gullet. Then stillness again, containment, as if it were there in its splendid isolation mostly to watch the morning break. The quintessence of poise.

Cove and sound, mountain and tree line, sky and sun, converge in the bird, wheeling around it. It is the morning's center point, the pivot of the universe. A phrase of T. S. Eliot's slips into my mind—"The still point of the turning world."

> ... at the still point, there the dance is,
> But neither arrest nor movement. And do not call it fixity,
>   Where past and future are gathered. Neither movement from
> nor towards,
> Neither ascent nor decline. Except for the point, the still
>   point, There would be no dance, and there is only the dance.

I feel the present, in which I have cowered for two heavy years, expand to dimensions beyond time. And yet the present is all there is, this stunned moment.

> Before the beginning and after the end.
> And all is always now.

To get to this still point of land, in time, has cost me everything.

The heron has moved up the strand. Herons nest in pairs but generally fish alone; this is a solo fisher, its solitude essential to its business and beauty. It stands for long spells at the shifting juncture of sea and land as if it were entirely alone in the landscape while connected to everything, occupying its place as a perfect single note occupies the air.

Eventually, the day begins to move.

ALWAYS/NOW

Later I root out the owner of the cottage and give her a deposit for a month next summer. It is not until the islands are behind me and I am back home that I recognize I have bought into the future—a small, rarified chunk of it, yes, but futurity it is. I have pledged that I will leave home again, and that I will look and live forward. I've put money on it, money I'm privileged to have. Through the dark midwestern winter I will carry in mind a tall, singular bird at the center of a morning.

I don't know that the heron my mother saw meant anything to her beyond the small thrill of seeing unusual wildlife in the suburbs. Its loneness may well have spoken to her. She may have carried it in her imagination, hoping to spot it again every time she drove down Fourteen Mile, but it's equally likely she forgot it. Her heron lodged in my memory, drawing meaning as my mother's life became clearer to me. It came to represent something singular in her, in every sense of that word, something apart from her circumstances. She was widowed twice, married three times, insisting that she was "a man's woman." But I always think of her as distinct and separate, and full of grace. What she wanted most for me was to be able to stand on my own in whatever winds blew through my life. So I try for that. I rummage through the jumble of myself for something like a bird balanced on the edge of time, patient as the sun, waiting for the approach of what it seeks.

BODIES OF WATER

The living walk by the edge of a vast lake
near the wise, drowned silence of the dead.

—Carol Ann Duffy, "Eurydice"

You slipped around the bend in the river, just past our property line. I wonder what caught you there, downriver—the neighbors' dock, tall weeds, a fallen tree? I can't think about that. The woods were filled with men in drab uniforms, lunging dogs, people in wetsuits who finally found you after an hour. Then another hour of trying to drive life back into your body. I can't think about that. And then, just past midnight, everything stopped. Stop. *Stop*.

✳

Water signs, both of us: you were Aquarius. "Slippery," you grinned. True: behind the convivial façade you were elusive, allusive, hard to grasp or hold still. You even spoke in codes. But Aquarius is not the water itself but the water bearer, bringer of life, douser of fires, quencher of thirsts. I am Cancer, awkward, overprotected, eye-beads peering out from under a carapace, scuttling away under the waves.

✳

I am sitting on a sunny rock high above a bend in the river, and you are wading downstream, casting out your line. You move across the singing current, into and out of shadow. You cast, watch the bobber ride the water, reel in; you turn, assessing the stream, and cast again. I see it all, your composure and stillness, your deep integrity. The landscape—high bluffs, shining sky, rushing water—coalesces around you.

Is this the day you tell me about the long, dark thing swimming upriver, coming straight toward you? You froze, and at the last instant it veered around you and moved on.

✳

In the blur of that night, I remember clearly standing at the edge, looking down the high bank, muddy and root-veined. Always I had found that bank a little scary, and now I knew absolutely that I was about to slide down it into the river. Because if I didn't, I could never say I looked for you. What if you were down there, just below me, and I didn't look? And so I sat and slid. The water was colder than I expected and the current swifter, seizing my feet. I slipped underwater, as if I might meet you there. But I knew better. I knew better before I left the bank. You were somewhere else. And this water was not where I belonged. A low tree offered a finger of a branch, and I took it. Once again the imperative: *You will have to live.* And the concession: *I will. I will.*

✳

I kept wanting the testimony of love, and always you offered the same story: you are coming off the river at the end of a fall day, wet and tired, creel holding a brown trout. You climb the bank and begin trudging back to your car, the ugly liver-colored Olds that rode so close to the ground I was afraid you'd bottom it out crawling back roads and over railroad tracks. And suddenly a wind raises a cyclone of leaves before you like a golden waterspout, whirling and dazzling, and you think of me.

And for you, that was the story. For a long time I heard it as a preface, wanting something more. Finally I understood: the light, the end of day, the weariness, the river behind you, the rapture of the leaves by the wind, my sudden appearance in your imagination—there was nothing else.

✳

Your body is what I cannot think about. I cannot think about your body in the air, having taken one step too far. I cannot think about your body in the water. I cannot think about your body in pain or terror. I cannot think about your body discovered downriver, retrieved, hauled up on land. I cannot think about them trying to resuscitate your body. I cannot think about why I didn't run to your body and touch you once more and beg you to breathe. But when a stranger called at 1 a.m. to ask what I wanted done with your body, I had to answer. Maybe I said that word *cremation* so that there would be no body for me not to think about.

✳

While you interviewed for a job all day in Marquette, I walked along the Lake Superior shore. It was a bright Tuesday, the eleventh of September, and that morning, back at the hotel, I had watched the flaming, gashed towers sink into themselves. Though the images replayed in my mind, it was hard to feel the calamity. The lake was deep indigo, as warm as it would get this year, running in small waves and lapping tamely at the stony strand. The edges of the thick trees were just barely gilded, but they would turn fast. Autumn is early and brief in this latitude. In just a few weeks the ice would begin to close in.

We wouldn't see each other until dinner. Then we could share what we knew about New York and Pennsylvania and Washington. I could look into your eyes and feel anchored to the earth. For now, I walked the water's edge and wondered: would we wind up here together for good? You had once lived here; what would it be for me? Who would I be this far north?

Tonight we had a cabin booked on a small inland lake. We would pick up steaks on the way out of town. We would watch the sun trail down across the water and drink gin, contemplating the world coming to an end somewhere else.

✳

Walking down the hall to the funeral director's office I try to pretend the big ugly house with its great-grandmotherly décor doesn't exist. None of this is real. This is only another space in time to get through. The man is much more upbeat than he has any right to be and I let my sister-in-law do most of the talking. I take in the model urns on the shelves, vaguely recognizing that someday I will probably laugh about the one with the antlers. This is northern Michigan. The man gives me more detail about cremation temperatures than anyone ever needed to know, as if the technicalities were fascinating. I wonder briefly if I am dreaming. Suddenly I think of your ring, your father's ring on your finger. *I can get that for you*, says the man and disappears downstairs. And then I understand that you are there, your body is there in the house with me, downstairs with other bodies, and a howl rises, starting small and growing, and I strangle it before it can ring through the dark heavy rooms of what used to be some well-to-do family's home in Kalkaska, Michigan, in the 1920s.

✳

I read it in the paper first, that the husband of an acquaintance has gone missing at Asylum Lake. The police have found cross-country ski tracks leading out onto the brittle early-April ice. A week goes by, and another, and still his body does not rise.

Although I do not know her well, I send a message. I hold a terrible specialized knowledge none of her friends will have. I never thought it would have a use.

She is Japanese, and I remove my shoes before entering her house. The house is spare and clean. We sit at the dining room table. She gives me tea and chocolate cookies. Our intimacy is at once tenuous and fierce. It is purposeful, pragmatic. She asks me questions about drowned bodies, autopsies, cremation, American funerals and funeral homes. About counseling, about grieving.

I know more than I tell her. I know water, how it draws bodies down and how it yields them up, and I know the dark place between, the hopeless waiting. Here in this quiet, sunny house, we speak while the April afternoon goes on at some distance. We hold tears just behind our eyes.

"Do you think I am a strong person?" she asks, as if I can provide some measure she can use. "I think I am a very strong person." We are drinking a pungent ginger tea she orders specially. She gives me two packets to take home.

I think we are all strong persons, for all the good it does us.

We have never before touched, but at her door we hold each other for a long minute. Outside I put on my shoes and walk to the car through the bright afternoon. I breathe it in. Spring, finally.

✳

The dark-gray vinyl container sits on a bookshelf in my living room. Occasionally I give it a sideways upward glance so that I don't learn to avoid it, endowing it with power. I wait for some idea to take hold.

And then one day, three years down the road, it's suddenly obvious.

With the container on the floor of the back seat, I drive for two days: around Lake Michigan into Indiana, around Chicago, north through Wisconsin into Duluth, and finally up the north shore of Superior toward the Canadian border.

On this August day the massive inland sea that broke the *Fitzgerald* like a stick is pond-placid, clear as a wide eye, warm enough to wade. Inside the gray container is a plastic bag. When I empty it into the water, a milky ring forms around me, widening then slowly sifting down to the clean red and gray stones at the bottom. I give you to the greatest of lakes, Mother Superior, the only thing I know that is big enough to hold you.

✳

Last night in a dream I returned to the river. I went there with someone else, to show where it happened. I was very calm, dispassionate. And as I'd expected, there was evidence: thin parallel lines, about two feet apart, down the bank to the water, as if I'd gone down on a sled; and next to the big white pine, some trace of where you went in, some object I didn't see clearly or don't remember. Maybe your slipper, as impossible for me to look at in my dreamscape as it was in wakefulness. I pointed out these traces to the person with me like someone conducting a tour of an interesting crime scene. I was miraculously whole and untouched, in a world where disaster leaves tracks and the earth does not forget.

THE MESSENGER

In a dream a few years back, I was walking from the kitchen of a house into its garage. From the corner of my eye I saw, up on a shelf or rafter, a huge white owl. It spread its great wings and swooped down on me, waking me to my own thudding heart.

I knew instinctively that the owl meant death. I felt it, heavy and powerful, coming for me. At this time I was well into middle age, lacking any real belief in the supernatural but always longing for it, as literary people often yearn for a world of symbol and meaning worthy of the one that words create. Despite knowing nothing then about owl symbolism, I was unnerved by the fierce clarity of the dream, the absolute specificity of the owl's direction. But my life rolled on. Then, a couple of years later, my mother, just shy of ninety, was suddenly unable to recover her breath. Something deep in her lungs resisted even analysis, much less treatment. At her firm request the tubes and machines were removed, and she died peacefully, as I held her hand.

Her death was breathtaking, exactly like the downward swoop of the owl. It swept the world like a sudden great wind. In its quiet wake, I contemplated my path. I considered the world without her, reeling without its axis. A week after her death I was driving north with Bob, heading to the cabin for Christmas. I don't think I had ever known such bone-deep exhaustion, the kind that settles in only after extraordinary tension abates. Watching the silvered fields and trees fly past, I thought how unmoored I was, how free.

Four years later, on an eerily dark New Year's Day, we were northbound again in the same car, feeling a slightly different kind of exhaustion. The previous morning we had been married. The sole shadow on the day, for me, was cast by my mother's absence. She'd probably resigned herself to my never marrying; she didn't seem to care much. But I think she would have enjoyed seeing her fifty-something kid walk down an aisle, particularly with a man she liked a lot.

We settled into the cabin and the long, white months passed quietly. One dark morning, as the winter began to melt, we were eating breakfast when Bob quietly said, "Look."

Outside the back door, on the deck, stood a big hawk. It was perched immediately over a chipmunk haven, biding its time. But it was staring straight into the house. Its obsidian bead of an eye was trained precisely on us. I had never seen a hawk that low, or that close. Until you look at a raptor that is looking back at you, you don't really know what it is to be *seen*. I watched, mesmerized, wondering what exactly it was that the bird saw.

That was March, I think. And then came the night in early May when Bob vanished and I felt my whole life drain out of me like blood.

✳

Five days later, back home in Kalamazoo, as my car was being unloaded, Scout came sauntering around the side of the house. He'd stayed downstate that year, in a house sitter's care. He acknowledged my return as he does, as cats do—with interest and the head rub around the ankles that plants scent, claiming us, which we translate as love. Nothing like the embarrassment of ecstasy a dog demonstrates. I remember bending to pet him— he hated being picked up—in a dreamlike state. I could manage minimal motions, minimal communication. "Scout," I said. "Hey, Scout," stroking his white head. He lifted his nose appreciatively. He was the most solid thing I had touched in days. And he was alive, and mine.

Call him my familiar. The *genius loci* of my homeplace. Nine years before, as a runty, starving kitten, he was rescued by a student of mine from slathering canine jaws beside a busy street. From the first, his personality was intense, an italicized version of the weird duality of cats: soft, comical, heat-seeking domestic creatures and strange, unknowable, untamed Others. One takes refuge in your house; the other resists his captivity. Scout was needy, affectionate, responsive, running home (if he felt like it) when I whistled and called him, galumphing downstairs to welcome me home. He was also diffident, elusive, grouchy, and potentially violent, suddenly going after my hand, teeth and claws bared, with zero provocation, ears laid back and nothing in his eyes but killer instinct. He emanated both the vulnerability and the feistiness of the runt. Through him I came to know yin and yang in some relation other than contradiction.

True to his bipolarity, Scout made it very clear from the get-go that while he was happy to have a home, he was not about to live his life indoors. I knew only that to keep him in cost both of us too much. He also quickly and firmly established that he was a hunter, hardwired to stalk and spring, stretch out and run low like a miniature puma. So, having put a bell on his collar to assuage my conscience, I recalled Tennyson's line about nature red in tooth and claw, gritted my teeth, and opened the door—over and over again. I applauded the mole and vole corpses, I lamented the chipmunks. But the feathers on the back step—those I grieved.

To "have" an animal: whatever it means, it means an intimacy with death—in that which our animals kill, or that which waits to kill them. Dog people are mostly buffered from it by all that trainability and unconditional love. Bird people keep it caged. Cat people see it in the eyes of their familiars on a daily basis.

✳

Four years after that surreal homecoming, as another lush summer broke over the upper Midwest, I was reading on the porch one night. Around 10:00, I looked up to see Scout tearing toward the house, his mouth barely containing something gleaming in the dark, huge and white. Bigger than his head. Almost bigger than his body. Before I could reach the swinging cat door, he sailed through it onto the porch, where he dropped a massive pile of pale gray and white feathers, facedown. He stalked around it, agitated, with that look in his eyes that I'd seen before after a kill: hypnotized. Not fierce or fiery, but entranced. As if he were seeing something eons beyond this night, doing the bidding of something invisible to both of us.

Over his protests I herded him into the living room and closed the intervening door. Then I bent to examine what I feared was (a) dead, or (b) waiting for its moment to fly into my house, or my face. I couldn't tell what bird it was or whether it was alive. It was at least a foot wide; I couldn't imagine how Scout got his little mouth far enough around it to carry it. Its feathers, lush and lovely, fanned out on its wings, opening precise zigzagging patterns of gray from pearl to dove to slate. It didn't move, but I saw no blood or breakage.

Only one thing to do.

I opened the porch door. Then, very gently, I slid my hands under the wings and lifted it. It filled my hands completely and spilled over. Silken, clean as if it had just been created, it may have been the softest thing I have ever touched. Despite its size it felt nearly weightless, like a cloud. Barely breathing, I slowly carried it outside and then raised it, even more slowly, high enough to look underneath.

The round white face of an owl, motionless, eyes closed. It had to be an adolescent: bigger than a baby but certainly not the size of an adult. I had never seen an owl outside of a book. It was stunningly beautiful. I wanted to look at its ghostly, peaceful face forever, but I was terrified—for it, of it. Who knows what an owl does when it regains consciousness after being traumatized? I laid it on the brick step as softly as I could, facedown again.

I went back inside, closed the door and shut the window with the pet door, released a very chagrined Scout onto the porch, and returned to my book. He paced around, mystified and anxious, sniffing the tile floor for some trace of his enormous achievement.

For a half hour I heard nothing but the usual noises of the night—crickets, car tires. I tried to concentrate on the page before me. Finally, a small ruffling, scritching sound—and then silence. I waited a few more minutes, closed the book, turned off the light, and went to the porch door.

The steps were vacant.

✳

If life were as mythic as it should be, I could anticipate a day when I would find myself in some kind of peril from which I would be rescued by a familiar-looking owl. But possibly some version of that was what happened on the porch. The night spirit Scout snagged was also the fatal white specter from my dreams. In the preceding years it had indeed come for me, in a variety of forms, finally in its own lustrous feathers. I had held life in my hands, seized from the jaws of death in the form of a small white cat who had once been similarly raptured. I had lifted it in love and fear. Something like prayer had pulsed in me as I handed it back to the darkness. When I heard its wings, I had felt a surging gratitude.

The association of owls with death and the dark side comes, of course, from their nocturnal character. From ancient times, and still in popular culture today, owls are figures of wisdom. In some sources you will find this duality labeled contradictory—the response of a culture terrified of death and given to stuffing complicated concepts into oppositional categories. As if wisdom and death were not intimates. As if wisdom were not a night-bloomer. The association with wisdom probably comes from Athena, goddess of wisdom, who took the owl for her symbol and companion because it could see in the dark—Athena, who was also goddess of war, her gray eyes keeping watch over death's playgrounds. In cultures respectful of the powers and truths of darkness, owls became messenger figures, bearing their night visions to the human world. Owls, then, become messengers, bearing unearthly news.

Or was Scout the messenger? His kind are also nocturnal and thus associated with the dark. As owls are to Athena, cats are to witches—wise women damned by the unwise. In the altercation of a summer night, the roles of cat and owl had been strangely confused: more often it is owls that seize cats. Beyond seizing it, Scout had had no interest in doing violence to the owl. He'd brought it to me, as cats do, with the urgency of one bearing momentous news, truth of heft and import. But the message was far beyond words, caught in the spinning double helix of death and life. I found myself in the presence of genuine mystery, where all meanings reside but none holds still.

As Scout and I climbed the stairs to bed, I still felt the weightless softness. How still the bird had been, holding its energy close until it was sure it could reenter its living. I felt its fierce, delicate life thrumming in me.

DEVASTATED

It's what everybody says they are now.
Your favorite restaurant goes out of business,
you're devastated. Your kid doesn't make
the swim team—devastated. Your one-nighter
fails to call again—you get my drift.
No one hears in it the cities burning
or sees the ruined fields. It means *laid waste*,
as in *Getting and spending, we lay waste
our powers.* Wordsworth, what's he on about?
I ask my class. Nobody has a clue.
They think he means we throw our powers away
like waste, like Styrofoam, or that we waste them
(whatever they might be, these obscure powers)
like money—not entirely wrong and yet
not right. Okay, try Jagger then: *I'll lay
your soul to waste?* Nope, nada. Later two
or three of them will say they're devastated
by their grade or someone's nasty text.
Words—what can we say about them? Slick,
absorbent, malleable, they mostly fall
apart. And then again, sometimes they hold:
two strange Englishmen, poised at the dawn
and dusk of the industrial West, imagine
the soul as ravaged, leveled landscape, void
of life or color, or of movement, save

the smoke meandering from exhausted fires.
I don't know how to tell you this story,
but if I say that for a certain while
I was devastated, I want you
to smell the fetid smoke, to see the dog,
starving and cankerous, nosing the waste.

POSTSCRIPT: BREATHE

One Christmas Bob gave me a small ceramic wall sculpture, the work of a Gold Hill neighbor. About a foot tall, it depicted a section of tree trunk from which a woman's face was emerging. Her eyes were shut, her lips parted as if she had been desperate for air and had finally found it. The entire thing was a steady medium blue tinged with gray. He told me it was called *Breathe*.

I hung it in our bedroom in the cabin. Two days after Bob died, after I had packed everything I had brought north for the year, I walked around the place, seizing anything I thought I might want or need. I made myself alert; I had to be thorough; I would not be returning here. I took the sculpture from the wall, wrapped it in newspaper, and laid it carefully at the top of a box of items I was taking away.

After I had been home a while and found the energy to unpack everything, I noticed the sculpture was missing. *Damn*, I thought, a box must have been left behind. Or maybe the sculpture was removed from the box by other hands, though that seemed very unlikely, and someone would have called by now. Now what? How could I retrieve it from a place I could barely think about? But I had to have it—breathing was not easy.

The cabin was on the market for two years before I got an offer, which I seized. I sold it at a stomach-turning loss at the height of the national recession, more like a depression in Michigan. The buyers wanted anything in the cabin that I was willing to leave—a huge relief, as I wouldn't have to sell things, which would have required me to be there longer than a day. Bob's son and his partner and I headed up one Saturday to clean the place and take what we wanted. Priority 1 for me was finding *Breathe*.

In the course of that long, grim day, I searched the cabin—every cupboard, drawer, closet, and box. The sculpture was nowhere.

But it has to be here.

I repeated the entire procedure, to no avail. It was getting late, Mike and Kris had already left, and I was exhausted in every part. I had worked nonstop, laser-focused, holding myself tight, and I needed to get out. Finally I gave up and left, locking the door behind me. Just as I began to pull away from the cabin, I spotted the wood-burned sign swinging over the front porch, the one I'd had made for Bob for our first Christmas here, when we felt so nervous about buying the place that we pledged to give each other only cabin-related items. The sign bore both our names, the cabin address, and a leaping trout. I couldn't bear to leave it. Feeling sick, I got out, unhooked it, and tossed it into the back of the car. Allowing one thick wave of pain to surge over me and exit in a sob, I drove away. Later I would burn the sign in my fireplace.

Okay, then, the sculpture has to be at home. Has to be, I thought. I clearly remembered packing *Breathe*, and I remembered putting the box in my car, with the sculpture buffered carefully on top. The next day I searched my small house again, everywhere. I called Linda, the sister-in-law who had harbored me in the days immediately following Bob's death, on the off chance I'd left a box at her house. No, she said, nothing.

I never found it.

It might seem easy for such a thing to vanish in the confusion following a disaster, with me in shock and family members and neighbors moving around the small space of the cabin, coming and going, moving and carrying and cleaning. But that process, though hurried, was not chaotic; in fact, it was remarkably orderly, even my part of it. The coil of my brain that can organize and execute like a bitch took over. I knew I would come back only once, to get the cabin ready to sell. Beyond that I never wanted to see the place again. So I was methodical about selecting things to take home. I carefully packed up the index cards and legal pads and books I was using for the book I was writing, with the cards grouped, rubber-banded by chapter and topic, and in order. I packed all my clothes except some socks I decided to abandon. I went through the kitchen cupboards and drawers and pulled whatever had meaning or might be useful at home. I took a lamp. I went through towels and linens. I surveyed the walls and took down everything I wanted, and that included *Breathe*. It was agonizing to lift it from its hook in the bedroom wall, but I knew it had to be with me.

Except it wasn't.

I am not given to supernatural explanations, but when I think through this mystery, I always arrive at one conclusion, almost by default: the one who gave *Breathe* to me took it back.

The problem is that I can't imagine why. I know he would want me to keep breathing, not to stop. In fact, when I was overwrought about something, he would say, simply, "Deep breathing..." When I realized the sculpture was gone, what it meant to me was that my breath was gone too—seized, as it were, by the river, as his was. Why would he inflict such a message?

Now the sculpture hangs in my mind, a constant, potent absence. I see it clearly: the rippling bark of the blue tree, the woman's emergent blue face, lips soft and open to the air. I feel her relief, muscles relaxing as oxygen floods them. I ponder her relation to the tree: did it entrap her, and is she now breaking free of it? Is she "of" the tree, the breathing spirit of it? Or have I read it all wrong: is she not coming out of the tree but sinking into it? Is she Daphne, the river god's daughter, turned by him into a tree so that she could escape the rapist Apollo? In the years since the sculpture vanished, the place it holds in my imagination has drawn other sorts of questions: *Are you breaking free? Are you a growing thing? What are you running from? If breath is spirit, are you releasing yours? Are you holding it in? What are you turning into, daughter of the strong brown god?*

Absence holds a power over presence. What is lost is insistent; it pulls at our attention more than the thing we hold securely (or so we think) in our hands. Even words themselves only name what isn't here, something we are chasing that has fled, so that writing, as Margaret Atwood has it, amounts to "negotiating with the dead." I keep missing the face in the tree, so I keep studying it in my memory. It is a kind of sphinx, refusing to give up its secrets. In a voice that is sometimes like his, absence whispers its name: "Breathe." And so that is what I do.

NOTES

Page

2   "I do not know much about gods": T. S. Eliot, "The Dry Salvages," In *Four Quartets* (London: Faber and Faber, 1941), 35.

18   The information on Gold Hill's history is taken from www.gold hilltown.com. Some details of the story of the inn come from www.goldhillinn.com.

36   The story of Annabelle Kindig Miglia can be found at https://themtnear.com/2012/08/40-years-later-kidnap-victim-tells-story, or in Miglia's book, written with Joyce Godwin Grubbs, *Footsteps out of Darkness* (Boulder: Annabelle, 2012).

58   On Linda Chase of Jackson, Michigan, and her longtime companion, Charles Zigler: *Jackson Citizen-Patriot*, July 11, 2012.

61   "wandering in a sea of people": Colm Tóibín, *Nora Webster* (New York: Simon and Schuster, 2015), 204.

63   "The deepening of the heart": Mark Doty, *Heaven's Coast: A Memoir* (New York: Harper Collins, 1996), 271–72.

66   "There are times I feel I'm translating": Doty, *Heaven's Coast*, 157–58.

69   "Write a poem in the voice of a widow whose husband has drowned": The title and all the italicized lines are from "The Widow," by Maura Stanton, an actual writing prompt included in *The Practice of Poetry*, ed. Robin Behn and Chase Twichell (New York: Harper, 1992), 60.

74   "I feel that we began witnessing the end of the world": Anne Lamott, *Plan B: Further Thoughts on Faith* (New York: Riverside Books, 2006), 17.

76   "grief constant as a twin": Jesmyn Ward, *Men We Reaped: A Memoir* (New York: Bloomsbury, 2013), 127.

Page

78 "All wise people say the same thing": Lamott, *Plan B*, 25.

88 "that awful slattern of the printed page": 1948 *New York Public Library Bulletin*, cited in the *Oxford English Dictionary*.

89 "a word or short phrase separated": www.desktoppub.about.com (accessed June 4, 2014).

89 "widows and orphans are words": www.wikipedia.com.

89 "An orphan has no past": *The Elements of Typographical Style*, 3rd ed. (Vancouver, BC: Hartley and Marks, 2004, 43–44).

93 "A widow is a word or line of text": www.opusdesign.us (accessed June 4, 2014).

105 "Each thing disappears": Doty, *Heaven's Coast*, 193.

113 "Deer playing about in great numbers": http://www.washington history.org/files/library/viewpoints-visions_001.pdf.

115 "very narrow and intricate channel": https://www.historylink.org/File/5060.

120 ". . . at the still point, there the dance is": T. S. Eliot, "Burnt Norton," in *Four Quartets*, 15.

122 "The living walk by the edge of a vast lake": Carol Ann Duffy, "Eurydice," in *The World's Wife* (London: Pan Macmillan, 1999), 62.

139 "negotiating with the dead": Margaret Atwood, *Negotiating with the Dead: A Writer on Writing* (New York: Cambridge University Press, 2002).

ACKNOWLEDGMENTS

I'm grateful to the editors of the following publications where these pieces first appeared, some in slightly different form:

"Heartbreak Hotel": *Full Grown People*
"A Creature, Stirring": *New Ohio Review* (2016 Nonfiction Prize winner)
"Bodies of Water": *MUSE/A*
"The Messenger": *Chattahoochie Review*. It originated as a much shorter piece in *Encore*, Kalamazoo's magazine of local culture.
"Devastated": *Southern Review*

My thanks also to the following people and organizations:

The Glen Lake Arts Council for a residency in my favorite corner of the world that helped me to write "A Strong Brown God";
Margaret deRitter, literary editor of *Encore Magazine*, for initially soliciting the piece that became "The Messenger," which is where this book began;
Sarah Einstein, whose painstaking line editing and rigorous critique made this a much better book;
Renée E. D'Aoust, who generously read an early draft of this book and sent extensive and encouraging responses, with chocolate, all the way from Switzerland;
the manuscript's first readers, Diane Seuss, Zaide Pixley, and Rachel Rosenfield Lafo, whose belief in me is crucial to me as a writer or as anything else.

My deepest gratitude goes to the people I call my Angels, who played a role in hauling me through grief's country and bringing this book to fruition. Whether they are named in these pages or not, I hope they realize that allowing myself to be cared for was a very important lesson I had to learn in this crucible. I remember every phone call, every kindness, every stalk of asparagus.

Finally, this book comes with great love to Bob's family—his children, Meredith and Michael; his sister, Breon, and her husband, Chuck; his brother, Brian, and his wife, Rita—who kept me in their hearts, before and after; and to Pam Poley, who walked every step with me for four years, providing safety, comfort, and wisdom, pointing me toward the land beyond grief's country.

ABOUT THE AUTHOR

Gail Griffin is the author of four books of nonfiction, including *"The Events of October": Murder-Suicide on a Small Campus* (Wayne State University Press, 2010), which anatomizes a student shooting at Kalamazoo College, where Griffin spent her career. Her award-winning nonfiction and poetry have appeared in venues including *The Missouri Review*, *The Southern Review*, *Fourth Genre*, *The New Ohio Review*, and anthologies including *Fresh Water: Women Writing on the Great Lakes*, a Michigan Notable Book.